# Facelifts Money & Prince Charming

## Break
## Baby Boomer Myths
## *&*
## Live Your Best Life

by

# Joanie Marx

Published by Sterling Media International, Inc.
ISBN-13: 978-1507765685
ISBN-10: 1507765681

Printed in the United States of America.

# Rave Reviews

*"Insightful, moving and extremely thought provoking."*

"In her wonderful new book, my former student, Joanie Marx, boldly confronts the mythical demons of scarcity, aging and abandonment with a refreshing and authentic voice. The book is insightful, moving and extremely thought provoking and will forever change the way you look at baby boomers and the generations that followed. With a distinct and inspirational style all her own, Joanie shows us all that life doesn't end after 55 – it's just beginning!"

~ **John Sudol,**
**Acclaimed acting coach and best-selling author of "Acting: Face to Face"**

*"Powerful and helpful in my own transformational journey!"*

"Joanie Marx has taken a subject that, until now, has remained taboo. I am actually from the generation after the Boomers and I found Joanie's story to be powerful and helpful in my own transformational journey! The wisdom and insight Joanie brings to some really bottom line issues of self-acceptance and self-love, are priceless tools for those who are committed to a path of self-discovery."

~ **Heather Powers, Singer/Songwriter/Transformational Coach**

*"New ways for baby boomers to examine their lives."*

"In her trailblazing book, I am proud to say that my colleague, Joanie Marx, not only courageously bares her soul in telling her inspiring story, but she creates new ways for baby boomers to examine their lives. Facelifts, Money and Prince Charming doesn't pull any punches and exposes the media's myths about the 55 and over crowd. As her producing partner on the commercial project, The McGranny Secret, I challenged her to share her truth in creating her Drive Thru Make it Your Own® campaign and that is exactly what Joanie has done in her book. With her own engaging style, Joanie reveals the truth about love, aging and creating one's own happiness as a baby boomer."

**~ Loren E. Chadima, Award-winning Acting Coach and Producing Partner and Director of The McGranny Secret Campaign**

*"Rewrites the story of baby boomers."*

"All actors – like all people – have a fascinating and inspiring story to tell. In her groundbreaking book, I am thrilled to say that a former student of Larry Moss Studios, Joanie Marx, not only inspires us to live our best lives, but she courageously rewrites the story of baby boomers by exposing the myths of our generation in a style all her own. Whether you're a baby boomer or you were raised by parents of this beautiful generation, this book will forever change the way you look at yourself."

**~ Michelle Danner,
Founding and artistic director of The Edgemar Center for the Arts**

*"Tunes out the voices of unworthiness."*

"I was talking about Facelifts, Money & Prince Charming with a friend recently and was asked what kind of book it is. I said, 'It's the kind of book that tunes out the voices of unworthiness that've been wreaking havoc on our lives all this time.' With a fearless approach to addressing the myths about the baby boomer generation, Joanie Marx has delivered a powerful pattern interrupt in how all generations think, behave and experience life. Thank you, Joanie, for having the guts to write a book like

4

this. You've courageously opened the door for a new, more exciting way to live for all of us."

**~ Peter Nelson,**
**Author and Unity Consciousness Activist**

*"An eye opening experience."*

"Even though I am not a baby boomer, Facelifts, Money & Prince Charming helped me better understand myself because I was raised by baby boomers. I grew up with the very same myths Joanie describes in her book. Being able to put a name to these myths made it a lot easier to identify and clear out thoughts about myself that I wasn't even aware of before. Her book got me to stop and think about just how much our parents and the era we grew up in influenced how we think of ourselves. We bought into what other people told us our Prince Charming is supposed to be. And most of us, including me, never had anyone say I am good enough just being me. This is a must read for anyone searching for that one, true love. Which, in this case, is yourself."

**~ Michelle Sheridan,**
**Professional esthetician and writer**

# Table of Contents

# Preface

How many times have you looked into the mirror of your soul and said:

I want to be valuable.

I want to be appreciated.

I want to be acknowledged.

I want to play and laugh.

I want to be loved.

I want to love back.

I want to enjoy being me.

As Baby Boomers, we understand the trials and tribulations of chasing the desires of our heart. But our path to fulfillment has often been blocked by seven myths that not only shaped our upbringing, but also served as a foundation for raising all generations that followed. These seven myths are:

1. Myth of Scarcity
2. Myth of Shame and Blame
3. Myth of Aging
4. Myth of Love
5. Myth of Prince Charming

6.  Myth of Self-Worth

7.  Myth of Physical Beauty

Baby Boomers have an inspiring and beautiful story to share. Such a story cannot be fully told, however, until we shatter the marginalized and fictionalized stories about love, aging and happiness that have been wrapped in these seven myths.

*NOT A HOLLYWOOD TALE*

Hello, I'm Joanie Marx and it is truly an honor to welcome you to the pages of *Facelifts, Money & Prince Charming: Break Baby Boomer Myths and Live Your Best Life.* Although I've been honored to play different roles on film and in various commercials, television programs and stage plays, this book is not a Hollywood tale. Nor is it written because I am unique. I am very typical of my time. Instead, the book is the result of my personal experiences as a Baby Boomer that were unexpectedly brought to life through the loveable and popular character, McGranny, I created to help launch the Baby Boomer advocacy campaign, *Drive-Thru, Make It Your Own*®.

The details of my life may be distinctly my own but I was not raised much differently than most of my generation.

As you will come to see with poignant examples of my personal journey, my life experiences, particularly those with my parents, are very much in alignment with millions of other Baby Boomers, just as they are relevant to the generations who came after us. As a proud member of the Baby Boomer generation, I am not alone in my need to feel loved and recognized for who I am and appreciated for my accomplishments. As a collective generation, we feel the forces that want to marginalize and stereotype our public presence. This does not make us different from other generations who are heavily influenced by the media, advertising and entertainment industries. What makes the Baby Boomer journey distinct are the myths, beliefs and rules that shaped the time period we grew up in, which dramatically impacted all future generations.

Because of our size in the population, and given the uniqueness by which Boomers are still physically and financially active in society, we can stand our ground and forever change how all generations navigate the emotional twists and turns of love, abandonment and aging that weave through our lives. By acting upon what we now know about ourselves, coupled with the use of technology and social media, we have a window of opportunity to free ourselves from self-imposed limits, providing our family and future generations a blueprint for what it truly means to live our best life.

## REMOVING THE FAÇADE

Being aware of and undoing our attachment to the myths of the past is not so we can turn the history of our lives into a profit making, pop-culture and nostalgia-based revenue stream. Nor is the retelling of our lives designed for us to rehash our mistakes and dig up painful grievances, guilt and abandonment issues only to hide them again. We've done enough of this already as a generation.

The point of removing the façade these seven myths have held up is so we can look at the relationship we have with our parents, our individual selves and the world in a new light, which releases us from the limits placed on us when we were growing up. This frees us of the immense burden of guilt and regret we have consciously and unconsciously been harboring inside of us all these years, allowing us to see past the veil that hid the real beauty and love of our life, which is ourselves.

With that in mind, when you turn the last page of this book it is my deepest wish that you will look into the mirror of your soul and see smiling back at you, your own lovable self, saying:

I am valuable.

I am appreciated.

I am acknowledged.

I play and laugh.

I am loved.

I love back.

I enjoy being me.

I am my own Prince Charming In Shining Armor.

Joanie "McGranny" Marx

www.McGranny.com

www.JoanieMarx.com

www.Facebook.com/McGrannySecret

# Chapter 1

## ~ MY BLUE HEAVEN ~

*"And they all lived happily ever after."*
*Unknown*

Not even a full 24 hours into my quarantine, and already I longed to play outside, anxious for the German measles to go away. I am five years old and it is summer time. I should be outside playing around the peach tree. Instead of filling my stomach full of peaches I am full of the measles, compliments of Georgie. He is a year younger than me and lives next door with his family and older sister, Joann.

I am told I will need to be in the dark for a long, long time. Feeling so sick, I accept my fate because it is what my mommy and daddy tell me I should do. Patience, however, is not one of my strong suits, but resiliency is. So to pass the time I hum our family song, "My Blue Heaven", as I draw our home with the sun in the upper right corner of the blank sheet of paper. I color the house a light shade of green, followed by the drawing of our peach tree in the front yard. We have lots of birds in the yard. So I add more life to this reflection of my home with birds flying in the sky above the house and sitting in the peach tree. The birds love that tree and I love watching them. Unfortunately, I am unable to watch them on this day.

In my separation from the summer fun, I take comfort in knowing my parents and stuffed animal, Freddy the Frog, will keep me company during the long days of confinement in my dark bedroom. As anxious as I am for the measles to go away, I can hardly contain my excitement for nighttime to arrive. For it is in the evening that my parents and I engage in our nightly routine of singing and reading, which is as close to Heaven as I can imagine.

*PRINCE CHARMING LIVES IN MY HEART*

For as long as I could remember my father, Sam, would come into my room and together we would sing our song, "My Blue Heaven". He always arrived before my mother and made sure to add a delightful twist with some creative licensing on the lyrics. "Tillie and Me and Joanie makes three, we're happy in my Green Heaven." I was used to the changes he would make with the lyrics and he never failed to make me laugh, always delivering a smile to my face. My father would take this smile as his cue to leave, but not before I would receive a hug and we'd exchange our nightly, "I love you". He'd wish me a goodnight and my eyes would follow him as he exited the room. This is when my mother would enter.

My mother rarely joined us for the singing of "My Blue Heaven", but on occasion she would stand in the doorway and hum right along with us. More than just my mother, to me she was and remains the most amazing person I've ever known. Her absence in the singing department was more than made up in her reading of stories to me. Many of these were from Golden Books, which would form a blueprint for me, as they would for millions of other impressionable girls and boys of the Baby Boomer generation.

I so loved to lean against my mother, feeling her warmth as I looked at the pictures on the turning pages. It was here that I first came to know of Prince Charming. As I nestled against my mother, I listened to her wonderful voice and looked in awe at the colorful imagery of the beautiful girls waiting for their Prince Charming to notice and choose them. Prince Charming always saved the girl of his choice, and together they would "live happily ever after".

These wonderfully enchanting "My Blue Heaven" moments with my mother and father superseded the anguish of being saddled with the measles. Despite the temporary hold on my usual activities I could not fathom anything disrupting this perfect life of ours. At five years of age, I was already envisioning my own adult life unfolding in a beautiful fairytale. This perfect idea of life, though, would soon be shattered, as I would not be the only one in my family who was sick.

## I AM A GOOD LITTLE GIRL

"Joan, bring me the thermometer," my mother calls out for me from her bedroom. I immediately turn to Freddy the Frog and exclaim, "This is a big girl job, Freddy." I roll out of my bed and yell out, "I'm coming, Mommy!"

This is day four of my quarantine with the German measles. I'm feeling much better and more than ready to get back to my normal fun-filled summer routine. I rush into my parent's room, eager to help. My mother is lying in bed. She isn't moving and doesn't look so good. Last night she was absent from dinner and reading me my nightly story. Daddy assured me everything was fine and mommy was just tired.

I ask her quietly, "Are you still tired, mommy?" She can see the confusion in my eyes, and lets me know all is well. She directs me to go into the bathroom where I get the thermometer. "Thank you, honey. Now go back to bed." I tell her I feel much better, but she isn't having any of that and reminds me, "You have to stay in the dark, so you don't hurt your eyes. Having German measles is scary." I don't argue and head back to my room.

Back in my darkened room, Freddy the Frog and I anxiously wait for my father to arrive home. I perk up the moment I hear the door open. A few moments pass by and then I see him as he blows me a big kiss from my bedroom doorway. He disappears down the hall to my parent's bedroom. A few minutes later he emerges from their room to let me know, "It's time for dinner."

At the dining room table, my father doesn't say anything. I instinctively try to cheer him up and exclaim happily, "This is the best hamburger ever, Daddy. Thank you!" He doesn't smile. When we eat dinner, it is always the three of us, but

*Mommy and Daddy are going to throw me away. Why are they doing that, Freddy? I am a good little girl.*

since my mother's unexplained absence, it is just me and my father. He isn't talking. I know something is wrong, but I

16

don't know what to do or what it is. So, I just eat the hamburger and eagerly wait for a conversation to ensue. It never does.

Before we finish eating our hamburgers, there's a knock at the front door, and my father gets up to answer it. A man with a big, odd-looking machine enters our home. He and my father move into the other side of the house, where I hear my parent's bedroom door shut.

Later that night, I am back in my bedroom. I hear lots of people coming and going in the house. None of them come to my room. By this point, I know something is wrong with my mother. And I am convinced it is all my fault. I just know I got my mother sick. I couldn't keep to myself any longer. With Freddy the Frog tightly held in my arms, I tiptoe down the hall to sneak a peek into my parent's room. I see my mother lying in bed. Beside her is my father, hunched over in a chair, holding her hand. I can overhear their conversation.

"Sam, I don't know what's happening to me, but today when I rode the bicycle up to the drug store to get Joan's medicine, I felt something terrible tear away inside me. We need to discuss what will happen to Joan." My father nods his head in agreement.

"I want you to promise me, Sam, that you will send Joan to my sister, Sarah. I want her to raise Joan." My father doesn't hesitate with an answer and says, "Yes, I will." No more words come out of his mouth. Something unimaginable is happening to my mother and my father doesn't fight for me.

I run unseen back to my dark and silent room, jump on the bed, and hug Freddy with all my might. "Mommy and Daddy are going to throw me away. Why are they doing that, Freddy? I am a good little girl." Freddy understands my unspoken words. "I love my Mommy and Daddy. I do everything they tell me to do. I didn't mean to make her sick. I am so sorry." His shiny glass eyes look back at me with compassion and love that I need more than ever.

I vow to myself, "If I have my own things I will always be alright." Suddenly, something grabs my attention. Freddy and I are not alone. Feeling my world collapsing, I look down from atop my bed and see a writhing pile of snakes slithering across the floor of my room. I am frozen with fear. I open my mouth but no sounds come out. My only movement is to quietly clutch Freddy tighter as more snakes emerge out from under the closet door hissing, coiling and circling my bed. From then on, the imaginary snakes occupy the nighttime floor of my room. As an adult, the visual of the snakes go away, but the dread of abandonment stays.

## I LOVE MY MOMMY

My measles are gone, but so too is the nightly singing with my father, and story time with my mother. After what seems forever, I'm let out of my dark room. But, I don't know where my mommy is. And daddy doesn't say anything. Then one afternoon he surprises me and says, "We're going to visit mommy."

Arriving at the hospital, I hold my father's hand tightly, skipping all the way from the parked car to the hospital doors. Upon arriving at the front desk, I hear the nurse say that I am too little and I am not allowed to see my mother. I could make her sick. My father escorts me outside. He points out the window where my mother is and says if I keep my eyes trained on the high up window, he'll be sure to have her wave to me. He re-enters the hospital, leaving me standing there alone.

I excitedly await a sign of my mother as my neck is already starting to hurt by looking up the seemingly endless rows of hospital windows. Then, I see her waving. I am overcome with a mixture of joy and despair. I am delighted to see my mother, but I can't touch or hold her. Tears stream down my cheeks as I wonder if or when I will ever see my mother again.

Several days later, my mother is released from the hospital. Her arrival back home ushers in a new life and a whole new set of fears that would take a lifetime to reconcile. The day she arrives home, I am so excited that I burst out the front door

*The prospect of being sent away, cast out of my home and family, abandoned as if I didn't matter, forever changed my outlook on life and my own sense of belonging.*

to greet my mother and father. I am immediately halted by a booming symphony of adult voices all yelling out, "STOP!" One adult voice exclaims, "Don't touch her, Joanie!" And another claims, "You could hurt her." I love my mother and just want to be next to her. I would never hurt her, but I back away, wondering, "What did I do wrong? I love my mommy."

I'm told by my relatives that my mother is very ill and any commotion could hurt her. None of them, however, reveal any details about what exactly is wrong. One of my relatives forcibly takes my arm and moves me out of the way as my father carefully escorts my mother into our home. I watch despondently as they disappear into a house that doesn't seem so Heaven-like anymore.

## WELCOME HAS ONLY ONE "L"

Eventually, I am allowed to see my mother. I am careful not to touch her, which is difficult because I want to hug her and be close. She looks upon me with tired, almost lifeless eyes. That sparkle I so vividly remember is now gone. "You almost didn't have a mother," she says slowly. These words echoed through my childhood, haunting and controlling me in ways I would not come to fully realize the extent of until the writing of this book.

A few days after coming home from the hospital, my mother is able to get up and move around. Prior to her return I carefully write, "Wellcome home" on the blackboard in our kitchen. Upon her first steps in the kitchen, I stand there proudly awaiting her reaction to what I had written. She enters the kitchen, glances at the board and then trains her sights on me saying, "Welcome has only one "l" in it." And with that she walks out of the room. I am left standing alone, my now tearful eyes fixed on my writing, incapable of understanding the rising tide of emotions forming within my being.

Everyone I knew had brothers and sisters. Not me. I didn't have anyone. What relatives I did have were incapable of filling the emotional void. It was apparent to me that my mother and father's priorities had drastically changed. And there was no adult to give an explanation, answer my questions, or offer a comforting touch.

After her illness, I no longer stood in the sunshine of my mother's smile. The threat of not having a mother, one who could die at any moment, and the chilling realization that I had a father who wouldn't fight for me became my new reality. The prospect of being thrown away, cast out of my home and family, abandoned as if I didn't matter, forever changed my outlook on life and my own sense of belonging.

*THE SCARS OF ABANDONMENT*

If a tree falls in the forest and there is no one to hear it, does it still make a sound? Feeling profoundly abandoned as a child is much the same. It means there is no one to hear our cries and no one to comfort our injured soul. We can all relate to abandonment, as no one is immune. Abandonment leaves behavioral scars, but it is not easy to look at the immense internal damage it causes. It's a dark space so bleak that few would dare travel into it again. As hard as it may be to face the moment of abandonment, we have to return to that space in order to free ourselves from the guilt and shame that comes from believing we did something wrong.

It would not be until I reached adulthood that I learned what it was that nearly took my mother away during that fateful summer. By then the damage of believing I was the cause of my mother's sickness had been done. It turned out to be a benign tumor on her ovary that

*Baby Boomers, as we were labeled, are a collective group of beautiful souls who have reinvented the idea of youth, but to this day remain in search of a youthful innocence that seems to have left us long ago.*

attached to her intestines and then tore away causing peritonitis and gangrene to set in. After the emergency surgery, her life still hung in the balance for the next three days. The lack of information given to me about my mother's potential life ending condition added to the

23

emotional scars of believing I was somehow responsible for what happened. Not unlike other parents of my generation, my mother and father provided little to no information about their lives. This lack of knowing left me isolated in my own fragile world to come to conclusions about my mother's condition and my own life, none of which filled the void that had been left during that fateful summer.

The effects of abandonment will be felt and projected into every facet of our lives until we courageously return to that moment and release ourselves from our attachment to the source of the pain we carry around. The source of our pain isn't something most of us are even consciously aware of because we have been raised to perceive the cause and solution to our suffering as being outside of the very place it exists. Until we summon the courage to pull back the curtain that hides our true selves, we will continue to mistake the void we feel within us as something that can be fixed from the outside. It is here, in our journey within, that we heal the scars of abandonment, rediscover a lost innocence and reunite with our inner Prince Charming.

Whether it was a person, job or any number of materialistic items we sought out for our fulfillment, the conceptualization of Prince Charming became a symbol for a lack of self-love. Our idea of being loved and acknowledged was placed in outside pursuits, other people and accomplishments, each of them representing an all-encompassing savior whose mere presence is believed to magically transform our life into a fairytale and prove, once and for all, that we are worthy of love. This is far from true.

I had no idea I would spend the rest of my life searching for ways to rebuild "My Blue Heaven" by looking for a Prince Charming to fill the void created in my heart. I often fantasized about being part of the fairy tales I would watch in movies and read in books, dreaming of returning to a place of safety and acceptance that seemed more like a distant memory with each passing year of my life. In doing so, my life would come to symbolize my generation.

## CHANGING THE WORLD

Baby Boomers, as we have been labeled, are a collective group of beautiful souls who have reinvented the idea of youth, but to this day remain in search of a youthful innocence that seems to have left us long ago. Like the metaphorical carrot that is dangled in one's face as an incentive to work harder, that elusive sense of belonging and acceptance always appeared within our grasp. With each accomplishment, though, we were painfully reminded that nothing we did or achieved would adequately fulfill us. This insatiable desire to be seen, heard and acknowledged fueled our search for love and acceptance in a world where it appeared there wasn't enough happiness and love to go around. Whether perceived as good or bad, the ways and means of finding our place in society would come to profoundly change the world. This change came with a hefty price.

The transition from our youthful adult years to the 55 and over club became perhaps the greatest challenge of all. Could we surrender our youthful attachments and modify how we perceive ourselves in the world as we grew older? One

> *"If you change the way you look at things, the things you look at change."*
>
> *Dr. Wayne Dyer*

of the greatest lessons we would learn along our journey can be summed up by author Dr. Wayne Dyer, who wrote, "If you change the way you look at things, the things you look at change." For a generation who spent the better part of our lives in search for something that could never be found outside of us, the understanding and application of this lesson is easier said than done.

Even though certain attributes of our physical youth are long gone, if we are to ever reclaim our lost innocence and discover that our true Prince Charming is within us, it requires a reconfiguration and reinterpretation of the values, rules and myths we were raised on. For today we are no longer seen as a youthful or relevant generation, let alone one that still operates at a high-level of alertness and competency. It is necessary for us, then, to change our perception about who we are in a world that is now intent on perceiving us as slow, elderly and obsolete.

How ironic it is then, that we Baby Boomers spend our entire lives fighting to be accepted by a world we wanted to change, only to reach the age we are now and discover the world we changed to fit our image refuses to accept us on our terms? In that sense our lives really have come full circle as Boomers fight to stave off being abandoned yet again. It's enough to make us wonder, "What's the point of our lives?" But there is a point to our time here in this world. Unlike the first time we felt abandoned as children, which we were helpless to stop, this time we are in a position to do something about it. We may not be as fast as we once were, but we are far from elderly, slow and obsolete. Therefore, we are not done changing this world.

# Chapter 2

## ~ THE SEVEN MYTHS ~

*"Pay no attention to that man behind the curtain."*
*Wizard of Oz*

In the iconic film, The Wizard of Oz, Dorothy is instructed to follow the path of the Yellow Brick Road, where her dreams of returning home will be fulfilled by the great and powerful Wizard of Oz. She understood that to deviate from this path meant certain doom. To ensure her safe return home and live happily ever after, Dorothy buys into the myths of "the great and powerful Wizard of Oz", as well as the myth she is told about her own destiny. She wisely listens to the sage advice and guidance from her trusted companions, bravely thwarts the Wicked Witch's attempts to derail her journey and ultimately makes it safely past the gates of the resplendent Emerald City. What she finds at the end of the Yellow Brick Road, though, is a huge disappointment.

Dorothy's desired outcome had all but been guaranteed so long as she followed the rules, believed in the myths and honored the traditions of the world she was in. Despite having made it to the Emerald City, nothing she had been taught about the myths and rules of this world turned out to be true. But it wasn't because her trusted companions had openly lied to her. They too believed in the myths, having passed them on to Dorothy as the truth.

During her initial encounters with the Wizard of Oz Dorothy's requests are denied, her friends are frightened and humiliated by the Wizard and their dreams temporarily shattered, in spite of their courageous journey. What she and her companions had been through was of little consequence to the Wizard of Oz. By agreeing to Dorothy's request, he believed his power and position of authority would crumble because the myths and rules he helped sustain would be revealed as illusions, destroying the status quo. Remaining behind the curtain symbolized the Wizard of Oz's fear of not being good enough, which compelled him to maintain his lofty position in society. His fear was projected onto all who called upon him for help, including Dorothy.

Like many in our world who are committed to holding up a false façade through outdated rules and illusionary myths, the fear of losing power was a driving force for the Wizard of Oz to keep the status quo intact. He firmly believed any change would result in him being shamed and rejected, rather than exalted as an all-knowing authority figure, as he had been all of those years prior to Dorothy's arrival.

At her lowest point, Dorothy could have accepted the idea of being betrayed by false myths and believed herself to be a victim of her trusted advisors and the Wizard of Oz's crushing rejection. To her credit she did not hold grievances towards anyone, instead she extended compassion and gratitude to one and all. Dorothy never strayed from being in the present moment and in doing so, she fulfilled her purpose by finding within herself the inner strength and courage to break free from the myths and rules that had falsely governed the world she was trapped in. Accepting that she was worthy of her goals, irrevocably changed the way Dorothy saw herself. This empowered her companions with the courage to reinvent how they perceived themselves, reminding the Wizard of Oz to see in himself that his greatest gift was inspiring people to achieve what they wanted by believing in the power of who they are. In the end Dorothy's acceptance of who she was forever changed the Land of Oz.

Like the Golden Books we read as children, The Wizard of Oz was part of many enchanting fairy tales we were raised on. For our generation it was as much as what we saw on television and at the movies as it was what we heard on the radio or read in books. These powerful influences intermingled with the myths our parents and society said would lead us to a fulfilling life. The older we got, the more our generation came to painfully see a fulfilling life had more to do with pleasing others than it did with being pleased with who we are. Convinced that love would be ours if we pleased others, we gave up on who we were and lost sight of what it meant to please ourselves. Summing this up is a famous quote from The Wizard of Oz movie that says, "A heart is not judged by how much you love; but by how much you are loved by others." On the surface the quote sounds good, but underneath its carefully structured words is the myth about love. At the core of this myth is a belief that the only way to reach the enchanted land of fulfillment and experience true love is determined by how others perceive us. Here our self-

> *"A heart is not judged by how much you love; but by how much you are loved by others."*
>
> *Wizard of Oz*

worth is trapped in the opinions of others, which keeps us enslaved by the belief that pleasing others is the only way to be accepted and loved.

Author and Professor of Psychology at Stanford University, Carol Dweck, wrote that the issue with attempting to please people, "Arises when parents praise children in a way that makes them feel that they're good and love-worthy only when they behave in particular ways that please the parents." But what if the people we attempt to satisfy cannot be pleased? This failure to gain acceptance from people and outside experiences inevitably left us all swimming in the sorrows of abandonment.

*SURVIVAL OF THE FITTEST*

Not unlike Dorothy, we were instructed as children that if we wanted to survive our adventure into the world of adulthood, we needed to seek out and follow the wisdom and guidance of our elders. They not only had traveled down the path we were about to go down, but they also held the keys to the kingdom we would someday inherit. What we didn't fully grasp at the time was that the perspective of life from these authority figures was heavily skewed by the strife and loss our parent's and grandparent's generation incurred.

Unbeknownst to most of our generation, the myths passed down from authority figures as wisdom were filled with scarcity and reinforced abandonment issues. We heard some of the horror stories of what many of our parents and grandparents had gone through. What was difficult to grasp was the extent of their loss. The world they had grown up in was rocked to its core with death, destruction and suffering that resulted in the unthinkable loss of what was treasured and valued most, those they loved. As a result, they believed that by teaching their children to hide their emotions, they were protecting them from the devastating loss they had experienced.

As a collective generation we were carefully groomed to strive for a better life all the while being forewarned to be wary of love and refrain from an open expression of our emotions. In a world that was built on the belief of survival of the fittest, hiding our emotions was important to our stability, safety and well-being. And nothing was more important to our parents than the safe, predictable path of stability. The safest thing we could do was keep our expectations about love and success in check and follow the rules, which ensured our goals stayed within the narrow scope of what society expected of us. This, we were told, was for our own good.

What most of us didn't realize until much later is that our parent's idea of a safe, predictable and stable life, which we all adopted in one way or another, isn't all that fulfilling. A life of scarcity based thinking is anything but safe and predictable. The sheer volume of evidence to support this can be found in the number of wars, economic meltdowns and an alarmingly higher rate of divorce and suicide among Baby Boomers than in any generation in modern history.

The fear of loss from the two generations that preceded us was also extensive. The only way our elders saw a way to help prepare us for success was to construct a path that was paved with nearly impossible to meet criteria, harsh criticisms of our talents and skills and an overt disdain for any outside of the box thinking. To please our parents and society it meant we could not deviate from the path we were told to travel on. If we tried or openly questioned the myths the consequences were severe. Our emotions and desires were of little concern as the primary focus was to prepare us for a harsh world. It was not difficult to see in a society that believed in the survival of the fittest the weak were discarded and marginalized while the strong were groomed through a rigorous set of rules and myths to ensure a world of safety and comfort.

*LOVE IN ALL THE WRONG PLACES*

Beyond the spectacle of the story itself, there is a great lesson in The Wizard of Oz that correlates to the primary theme of this book. It's more than just pulling back the curtain on the myths and lies of

> *The true magic, and our one and only force of change, comes from within.*

who we are. The underlying message is to release ourselves from our guilt and shame of not being enough by accepting there is no magical force outside ourselves that can fulfill us. The true magic, and our one and only force of change, comes from within. But how do we know this to be true? And how can we accurately navigate our inner feelings after following a set of myths that turned out to be false?

Even if we didn't always believe our parents, it was hard to argue their point about scarcity and how harsh the world was. Our younger years were consumed with threats to our sense of peace. As the media, advertising and entertainment industries grew, so too did the stories about our safety being in constant peril. Everything we loved, we were told, could and would eventually be taken from us. We were raised in a world of abandonment.

The older we got, the more we believed the stories of scarcity were true and we adopted them to our way of thinking and living. In this way, our lives were literally no different from our parents; except we were driven by our need to earn our parent's respect and please them on levels previously not seen in their own generation. This meant we had to do better than they did. But, with every new improvement we ushered into our world, came an even bigger threat to our happiness.

Our creativity was driven by the myth of scarcity, so the more advancements we achieved the greater burden we carried and the further we felt from a fulfilling life. For those of our generation that broke tradition and defied the myths, passionately seeking to paint the world with rainbows and love, they were met with extreme prejudices, not just from the authority figures of the time, but from other Baby Boomers. Whether it was raging against the establishment or becoming part of it we became a generation whose beliefs in myths and fairy tales justified a passionate search for love in all the wrong places. It's time we gain clarity on the seven primary myths that have kept us running tirelessly in circles all these years.

## THE SEVEN MYTHS

1. ***Myth of Scarcity:*** The root of all myths. You cannot have all that you want because there is not enough abundance for everyone. Love, money, youth and happiness are fleeting, impossible to sustain and can be taken from you. The only way to safeguard yourself in a world of threats is to accumulate as much as you can and give away as little as possible.

2. ***Myth of Shame and Blame:*** Follow the rules, respect your elders and do not question authority. To question authority results in you being shamed and blamed into submissive silence. This myth protects the status quo, serving as the foundation for the fortress that keeps intact all other myths.

3. ***Myth of Aging:*** Aging is an ugly, painful and distasteful disease. Reinforced by the media, advertising and entertainment industries for over 60 years, getting old was sold to the world as the antithesis of being youthful. It is not sleek or sexy. The best way to avoid aging is to quarantine the elderly and keep them out of the public eye as much as possible.

4. ***Myth of Love:*** Love is fickle; it hurts and cannot be trusted. In a world of scarcity there is not enough love to

go around, prompting people to use the idea of love to manipulate others and take away what you value most.

5.  ***Myth of Prince Charming:*** If you follow the rules, you will live happily ever after. And the rules state that fulfillment is not within but outside of you. Thus, Prince Charming symbolizes your search to fulfill an inner void of abandonment.

6.  ***Myth of Self-Worth:*** The only way to be loved and appreciated is to please people. Whatever the criteria is to gain approval it must be met or exceeded otherwise you have little social value. The mantra of, "I am enough. I do enough. I have enough," was measured by what the media, advertisement and entertainment industries told us carried social worth.

7.  ***Myth of Physical Beauty:*** To be physically youthful and beautiful is to be loved, admired and wanted. Inner beauty is spoken of, but carries little social value. If perceived as unattractive and ugly, you are deemed undesirable, unwanted and easily discarded.

## ADDICTED TO THE STATUS QUO

These seven myths, and many others that were offshoots of them, reinforced the belief that there wasn't enough to go around. The ever-present fear of losing what we love produced an emotional disconnect between our true value and what society was raised into believing carried social value. This induced an epidemic rise in a variety of emotional, psychological and physical conditions in the Baby Boomer generation. The need to seek comfort, acceptance and love outside of us to get what we could before it vanished, created addictions on a mass scale the likes of which the world had never seen before.

If we questioned the validity of these myths, pointing out what they were doing to us, or attempted to circumvent the rules of scarcity based living, we were blamed for disrupting the status quo and shamed for doing so. Eventually the effects of living in the world during our era were impossible to ignore, giving rise to new industries that had never existed before, all of which were catering to our need to be loved and acknowledged. This only served to create more of a need to please others, while also prompting us to rebel against the very people we wanted acknowledgement and love from. So, what kept the mythical wheels turning in a society that was breaking apart at its seams? It is the addiction to keep the status quo intact. And what few will want to admit is that a central pillar that props up the status quo is the need for people to suffer.

In our own distinct way, all Baby Boomers rebelled against the status quo. It's not as if we just blindly followed along with everything we were told. For me, I purposely kept my room dirty to upset my mother and openly defied her whenever I could. But this rebellion ended up hurting me more than it served my intent to show my mother who is the boss of me. I sabotaged my ability to use phonetics to sound words out and be a good speller because I knew this angered my mother. While I eventually overcame this, as evidenced in my acting and writing, I can't help but wonder how I made it through the demands of studying at UC Berkeley during a time when I was still rebelling.

Although our generation rose up and made sure the world heard the dissenting roar of our voice in the 1960's and early 1970's, soon thereafter we allowed that voice to be silenced. We summoned the courage to speak up, but it was the swift and often harsh response from our parents and other authority figures that ultimately shamed and blamed us into silent submission. We begrudgingly accepted the status quo, which strengthened the very myths so many spoke out against. In doing so, we validated the #1 rule we were taught growing up, which is to not question authority.

*OUR MOMENT IN THE SUN*

Authority was the law, at home, school, church and the workplace. We did not trust anyone over the age of 30 which presented quite a challenge. Those in a position of power, who set the rules and upheld the standards we were expected to follow, were all over the age of 30. If we were going to make a change, we simply had to wait our turn. This we could do, because fueling our quest to break free from the stifling nature of the status quo, was our youth. As far as we were concerned we'd be always be young and the "old-guard" wouldn't be around forever.

Many of us believed once we got into the hallowed halls of power and influence, our youth would give us the power to change the world and alter the fabric of society. Our parents were the conservative generation; whereas we were the creative upstarts, the dreamers and thrill seekers. Our youth was a shield against all perceived threats, specifically those posed by the survival of the fittest mindset that followed us into adulthood. Regardless of our youthful exuberance, our parent's guarded ideas about love and belief in scarcity, coupled with society's fear of aging, had been infused in our psyche, influencing us in ways we wouldn't realize for quite some time.

Once it was our turn to assume power, and our generation had wrestled away the keys to the kingdom, we finally had our moment in the sun to bring our youthful, creative ideas to fruition. We did in ways no one could have imagined. But, under the sleek and sexy image of our newfound success, the inner sanctum of our lives remained eerily similar to that of our parents. Whether we admitted it or not, the myths and rules we openly rebelled against we were passing on to a new generation as the blueprint for living a fulfilling life. Unlike our parents though, we knew these myths and rules did not work. But, we upheld the mythical ideals we had grown up with because we had been taught that disrupting the status quo brought about pain and suffering. In an avoidance of more pain and suffering for ourselves and others, we passed the seven myths onto the next generation, as our parents had done with us.

Could it be that in all of the vast achievements of our generation, we became as frightened by society and as guarded about love as our parents? The fear of being shamed and blamed for standing up for what we believed in stopped so many of us from living an authentic life we knew we deserved. We may have been a generation that let loose and partied, but we also became a generation that couldn't let go of the need to be people pleasers. In denying ourselves the freedom to cut loose from the myths of our past, we ended up pleasing no one and quite possibly squandered our youth. Without acknowledging what we had within us, we became a generation that sought out anything that could do for us what the Ruby Red Slippers did for Dorothy; take us to the home of our innocence.

## IN THE MIRROR OF NOW

We once looked into the mirror of our soul and believed youth was forever. It never really occurred to us we'd grow old, because we had our youth to protect us from this perceived disease of aging. But what about today? Do we fear looking into the mirror of our present reality, unwilling to see the reflection of our soul as we once did?

Dorothy's iconic line from The Wizard of Oz, "There's no place like home," speaks to our unquenchable desire to return to that mythical space in our heart where safety, comfort and love await us. This is

*"There's no place like home."*

*The Wizard of Oz*

where all symbolic references to Prince Charming come together, leading us to one singular feeling where we are fulfilled and safe at home. But where is the place we feel safe, fulfilled and at peace? Is it in the meaning we place on our relationship with the outside world? So long as we continue to believe in the myths that we were raised on we will remain committed to seeking our validation and sense of self-worth outside of who we are.

In our search for fulfillment we are taught to identify our strongest desires and proceed to set goals and a plan to manifest these desires into a physical reality. The goals themselves are not the real prize. It is the feelings we get when a goal is achieved that we are going after. But what is the meaning we give to these feelings? How and where must we gain our sense of fulfillment and validation for a job well done?

There was a time when nothing could convince us we weren't going to achieve our goals and be fulfilled. Once we began to accomplish even a few of our lofty ideals it became apparent we were not as fulfilled as the myths led us to believe we would be. What happened? Is it true there isn't enough love and happiness to go around?

Perhaps we accepted defeat at the hands of time and cynically give up on our desire:

To be valuable.

To be appreciated.

To be acknowledged.

To play and laugh.

To be loved.

To love back.

Given what we've been taught about the myths of love, aging and scarcity, could it be true that we bought into the idea that our ships of desire have long since sailed away with our youth? With so many false myths and lies told about Baby Boomers through the media, advertisement and entertainment industries can any of us legitimately say we know enough about ourselves to answer that question? And if we do, can we accept who we are today by letting go of these nostalgic ideas about the youth of our past, which distract us from the youth we are enjoying today?

It's time to let go of the stranglehold the Baby Boomer myths have had on us so that we can see who we truly are. It's time we go home. And by home, I mean going inward and seeing within us right now the beauty of our youth we believed was taken from us long ago. For, we are younger now than we will ever be in any of our days to come.

# Chapter 3
## ~ UP CLOSE AND PERSONAL ~

*"The tragedy of life is not that it ends so soon, but that*
*we wait so long to begin it."*
*W.M. Lewis*

In the next few moments I have to decide if I'm going to kill my mother. I've never killed anyone before. I try rationalizing all that she and I have gone through over the years and surprisingly, I came up with some compelling reasons to go one way or the other. But, as convincing as some of them may be, I'm left unprepared. It's not every day that people are faced with killing someone they love, or is it?

The inescapable truth is that my mother's doctors have presented me with a decision I did not ask for. I am faced with is the unimaginable pain of killing my mother. More than my mother, she is and will forever remain my best friend and the person I loved most in this world. No sooner do I feel my heart swell with the joy of loving her that I also feel my stomach drop with the dreaded inevitability that however this turns out, my life and hers will never, ever be the same.

Despite the sense of urgency with having to make this decision, I am stuck with trying to understand a series of thoughts that keep flooding my already overwhelmed mind. Even now, when killing is up close and personal, as it is for me in this moment, I find it impossible to escape the thought that of all human traits, killing is perhaps the least foreign concept in our world.

I tell myself I am not alone in this belief as my generation has numbed itself to the emotional impact killing has on the quality of our lives. In a relentless pursuit of believing our happiness is outside of us we have somehow justified killing in order to attain whatever Prince Charming may symbolize for us in the form of safety, comfort and fulfillment. We have mastered the art of desensitizing our natural aversion to death by learning to rationalize and justify killing in all of its various incarnations so that we barely notice it. Everywhere we look, someone or something is being killed every minute of every day. Boomers are, after all, born out of the death and destruction of World War II. And every war of every kind since then has been televised, reported, dissected and discussed more openly than any time in history as nightly news on the television and Internet news sites are filled with stories on death, delivered in high-resolution imagery at comfortable, disengaged distances. But there is no safe distance for me to hide from in deciding whether my mother lives or dies.

No matter how I try and shift my focus around these ideas about death, memories of my life with my mother are racing through my mind at a breakneck pace. I am torn between a deep appreciation for life and a gravitational pull toward the avoidance of pain. That is really what killing someone is all about. It's the release of pain. The avoidance and release of pain is the impetus that sends us on a shopping spree through life to acquire anything and be with anyone that can keep us in the good graces of society's impossible to satisfy definitions of what it means to be happy. But right here and right now, I cannot go on a shopping spree. No special someone to lean on. No cosmetic surgery and no amount of money will help. No manufactured Prince Charming will save me. No, this is all on me. I am petrified.

*HOW DO I KILL MY MOTHER?*

I cannot bear the pain of watching all that my mother was disappear into a ghost. Due to her deteriorating condition my mother may not be feeling the pain as I do, but somewhere in the loss of control over her life there is an undeniable truth. She is no longer the mistress of her own fate, as she was so fond of saying most of her life. And I am no longer capable of hiding from the reality that I am about to be alone.

Making a decision to kill a loved one isn't really a choice but more of an acceptance. Things like this can't be rationalized. Once you get this far down the path, the only choice left is to accept the choice that was already made. That's how she and I got here. This is when I recall the young doctor looking through my mother's recent tests and concluding, "We've let this go on too long." As much as I fought this, I couldn't ignore the reality of it anymore. He's right. But how do I accept that he's right? How do I know I can do what is being asked of me and not feel the unimaginable pain from believing I have ended my mother's life as much as I was feeling my own life was ending?

The closer I get to accepting I'm going to kill her, the harder it becomes to justify going through with it. And yet, I cannot seem to come up with any reason that's not selfish for going one way or the other. Feeling guilt for any decision I make is nothing new. Growing up, my mother made sure of that. Despite what I felt were my shortcomings and however I chose at times to blame my mother for them, the reasons for not killing her are becoming increasingly outweighed by why I should.

## A CRUEL IRONY

The cruel irony of life is that in our attempt to connect with others, we hide who we are and end up disconnecting from ourselves. This illusionary distance between who we are and who we think we want to be, creates the pain and suffering that none of us want to look at, but inevitably cannot hide from forever. As we have danced with our fears of self-love, our temporary sense of self-worth is projected onto everything from facelifts, loveless marriages, joyless jobs, money and anything we can use not to face the harsh realities of our guilty pleasures of denial.

> *The cruel irony of life is that in our attempt to connect with others, we hide who we are and end up disconnecting from ourselves.*

No matter how far we run from who we are or all those places where we choose to hide our denials of self, there is but one reality we cannot escape. Every Baby Boomer will have to face the death of a loved one, including our own selves. In some cases, such as my own with my mother, we will be placed in an unenviable position of making a decision to kill a loved one. Try as we might, we cannot get away from our emotions in this situation. Even for those who attempt to remain detached and rationalize death will be forced to get real. For a generation who has spent so much time avoiding reality, this life-altering decision is quite the wake-up call in our quest to face and accept who we truly are.

## *OUT WITH THE OLD, IN WITH THE NEW*

It is no secret that aging is not respected in our culture and neither is dying. As we age, we all fear being cast out for something or someone younger and better. The idea that we are becoming unseen, unchosen and discarded is scary and downright sad. An underlining premise of this belief is the famous adage, "out with the old and in with the new." The advertising and entertainment industries run on this premise. No company wants to be perceived as out of touch with the times. Even the oldest of products and their marketing messages receive makeovers as companies reinvent their brand to fit the tastes and interests of that elusive younger market. The companies that are doing all they can to not be forgotten, unseen and discarded are in essence not unlike Boomers. In one way or another we're trying to avoid death. But is this a healthy endeavor?

The resources, both financially and emotionally, we place in staving off the aging process, which includes the avoidance of death, causes enormous strain. This is where the chase for Prince Charming takes a dark turn. We seek outside distractions to create a false sense of security and happiness, which cannot last. It is an avoidance of a future that will not have us in it at some point. For a generation that redefined the idea of prolonging youth this unavoidable reality is not an easy thing to digest.

> *The companies that are doing all they can to not be forgotten, unseen and discarded are in essence not unlike Boomers. In one way or another we're trying to avoid death.*

When we were younger our generation steadfastly believed we'd always be young, so why worry about aging, let alone death? Those were our parent's realities and concerns, not ours. Soon, however, it became evident that we were not going to be as young as we once were, no matter how much we resisted it. Death has become an ever-increasing reality for Baby Boomers, be it the loss of our spouses, friends, and family members, or the heightened concern for our own health issues. Our inability to face our temporary place in this world ultimately robs us of the joy of what we have in our lives right now.

It sounds absurd to speak of aging like this in a time where we seem to know so much more about the value of life and how to prolong and appreciate it. It's true that Baby Boomers are certainly more active in all social arenas than previous generations. And we are enjoying a healthier and more vibrant lifestyle than any generation before us. But, it is important to remember how society has framed its perspective of life around the myths of aging and the scarcity mindset that says there's not enough love and happiness to go around. If we are not careful these very same myths we were raised on will continue to be passed down to each generation as the truth long after we are all gone.

We were not taught how to deal with our parents dying or how to face our own death, because most of our parents rarely spoke about such things. Left in the dark to form our own opinions, we had little to go on but the fantasies we were being told about life and death. The myth that aging is a disease and how growing old has been communicated to the world through the media, advertising and entertainment industries cannot be overstated here. And the truth of who we are cannot be kept in the dark any longer.

It's very easy to forget we once lived in a world without access to the volume of information we have today. Our perception of the world was originally created through a very narrow window of knowledge, which created a narrow point of view on life and death. Many Baby Boomers still carry this unchanged viewpoint today, which influences a great number of people. It is up to us to show the world that scarcity is a myth, aging is not a disease, and there is enough love and happiness to go around. As difficult as death may be to face for any of us, it too is not something we should fear. But, this is much easier said than done. So, perhaps the greatest gift we can give to ourselves and others is the permission to stop running from the one person who can help us enjoy our life while we have it. And that person is our self.

# Chapter 4

## ~ TIME FOR A CHANGE ~

*"I came into this world to be myself. For that I came."*
*Joanie Marx*

Around a lunch table this book was born. My college sorority sister, now a widow, lamented that she would never find a new mate because she didn't look young enough, had never undergone a facelift, nor had enough money to attract and bankroll a suitor. Therefore, according to her, there was no Prince Charming in her future. Mind you, this was coming from a bright, educated and pretty woman. How could she think like that? How could someone who is greatly admired see herself as a discarded old woman, without a shred of hope of finding a new love?

This wasn't the first time I witnessed fellow Baby Boomers express their dissatisfaction with love, or heard people use age as a means to discredit their lives. But this was the first time I was appalled by it. Where did such an idea about aging come from? How could we have created an environment that leaves its women and men feeling less than the beautiful and loved people they are just because of their age, physical looks, or the size of their bank account?

I've been subjected to age discrimination myself and now I was seeing the myths about love and aging play out in the lives of my dear friends on a level I had not previously imagined. I would soon come to realize these limitations my friends spoke of are a daily reality for millions of Baby Boomers, particularly women. This was something I could not stand by and accept. Leaving the luncheon that day, I vowed to do battle against these myths that so deeply affected my friends and fellow Baby Boomers around the world.

## FOLLOW THE GOLDEN SCRIPT

My life profoundly changed in my late forties and not by my design. But still, it set me on the path to find my inner Prince Charming and to be my authentic self. First, I had to sort through the legacy of my parents, especially my mother's perception of me, which was conveyed in a not so subtle message that if I followed her rules everything in my life would be perfect. As an only child, I always felt like I was on the outside looking in, and everyone else had a better life than I did. Growing up I had no idea my mother's perception of me was similar or even exactly the same as how society, and other parents of our generation, perceived their children.

As I surveyed the landscape of my generation, it became very clear to me what shaped Baby Boomer myths is not an isolated incident for a select few. These myths affected all of us growing up and to a large degree, still do. Our parents taught us these lessons: You are good and valuable because you please me. You are selfish and bad if you don't follow my script for you. Follow the Golden Script and Prince Charming

*Our lives were defined by how much we pleased others and less about how pleasing our lives were to ourselves.*

will come and save you. This promised "happily ever after" ending was frustratingly elusive for most of us. And even for those who seemed to have fulfilled it, most will tell you that beyond the exterior of their fairytale lives, there is a void that seemed impossible to define, let alone fill. For a generation that appeared to achieve so much, why does it feel as if we have done so very little? Is there anyone among us who hasn't accomplished a major life goal, only to be left wondering, is this it? Is this what life is all about? Could it be possible that we reshaped a world to fit our youthful image, only to be dissatisfied with what is reflected back to us in the mirror of our current age?

My mother's predominant message encapsulates many of the myths covered in this book. Growing up, I interpreted them to mean that by being the ideal, loving daughter and devoting myself to who she wanted me to be, guaranteed my dreams would be granted. I would be the good girl, get the husband I am supposed to have, follow him with faith and trust and live happily ever after. Instead, I found myself on the path of enchantment lost.

It wasn't that my life turned out badly, or that I am somehow resentful for how my parents and society influenced me. We were not raised to drive through life and make it our own. We were told to make our lives fit within a confined, cookie-cutter life that made our parents and society feel safe. Our lives were defined by how much we pleased others and less about how pleasing our lives were to ourselves. Herein lies the gap between the fairytale we were told was ours and the reality of what we've had to painfully adjust to and reconcile through our adulthood. It is here that the underlining goal of this book is framed, which is to break the myths that tell us happiness and fulfilment can be found in anyone or anything outside of us. We are, after all, our own Prince Charming.

*RETRACING MY STEPS*

After lunch with my friends, and upon taking a closer look at how Baby Boomers are perceived in the media, advertisement and entertainment industries, I couldn't sit on the sidelines anymore. I felt compelled to do my part to change the awareness the world has about us. Most importantly, it was time to change how I see myself in the world. This meant I needed to retrace the steps of my own life, looking at the myths that shaped me, and then see how they correlated to others from my generation. Mind you, this was not an easy task. It required me to look beneath the surface of my experiences and go deeper within than I had dared to even think was possible.

In late 2012, I began rewriting the story of aging and breaking Baby Boomer myths through the McGranny character. It started out as an idea aimed at changing the perception for how Boomers are portrayed through the media, advertising and entertainment industries. What unfolded from that initial idea and what it has turned into is far more than I had ever imagined. McGranny isn't the voice of one person or even a single generation.

The message of the *Drive-Thru, Make It Your Own*® advocacy campaign reverberates across all generations, most of whom will someday find themselves in the 55 and over crowd. To reach the audience this message resonates with it was important to utilize online and offline platforms that could distribute inspiring, humorous and thought provoking content to reinforce the idea that Baby Boomers are a powerful and influential force to be admired, respected and genuinely honored. Videos of me as the McGranny character were released through YouTube. Three spec-commercials were produced and filmed, showing a new and refreshing way Baby Boomers can be portrayed in advertisements. The response was overwhelmingly positive.

By the spring of 2013, I was being interviewed on multiple radio programs and publishing excerpts of what was developing into the book, *Facelifts, Money and Prince Charming: Break Baby Boomer Myths and Live Your best Life* on Facebook at: www.Facebook.com/McGrannySecret. While I had no idea what to expect from all of this, I instinctively knew what I was being called to do extended far beyond the initial idea for McGranny, let alone the pages of any book. The culmination of all the work that went into the campaign and the feedback from Baby Boomers all over the world was quickly reshaping the original framework of the book. All of this was quite overwhelming and at times I just wanted to stop.

By the fall of 2013, it had become quite apparent that not only had this campaign struck an emotional chord with people, but this was just the start of something much more than how we were portrayed in the media, advertisement and entertainment industries. Within the context of a rapidly changing world, I began to see the essence of this book and its timing represented a wake-up-call for me as much as it was part of a global wake-up-call for all of us to break free from the limits of our past. If we are to truly make our mark on the world, it won't come by how we define ourselves from outside pursuits or from the nostalgia that so many look to as a definition of the times we grew up in. It will come down to how we see ourselves from the inside out.

## *PEOPLE PLEASERS*

Although it was likely never said to us in this way, our pursuit of Prince Charming, in all of the various forms this mythical idea took shape, was directly linked to pleasing other people over ourselves. We were taught that to love ourselves is selfish and the only way to be happy is to acquiesce to the wants and desires of others. Our lives have been so consumed with pleasing others, that no matter what we did it was never enough. Abraham Lincoln once famously summed up the plight of our generation way before we came onto the world stage when he said, "You can please some of the people some of the time, all of the people some of the time and some of the people all of the time. But you can never please all of the people all of the time."

Our insatiable desire to find love outside of ourselves by pleasing others has been the underlining basis for how Baby Boomers were raised to define their self-worth. The way we saw ourselves became a mirror for society as we reflected the world we were raised in. If we failed to land our ideal mate, didn't secure the big break in our career, couldn't afford that trendy product, have the ideal physical appearance, or we came up short in the achievement of a goal, our lives were anything but joyous and the feelings of abandonment were front and center. Operating under a belief that if we followed the rules and achieved the goals others set for us, we'd reclaim all that was lost in the trauma

> *"You can please some of the people some of the time, all of the people some of the time and some of the people all of the time. But you can never please all of the people all of the time."*
>
> *Abraham Lincoln*

63

of abandonment. So, we kept repeating this vicious cycle of chasing for acceptance and love outside of us, thinking that somewhere along the journey we'd finally please everyone.

Where did these feelings of our lost innocence and not being enough come from? And why did so many Baby Boomers grow up feeling as if we had been abandoned well into our adulthood? Most of us were brought up by well-meaning parents, who did the very best they could with what they knew. Many even pointed out that happiness is within us. But, what they knew and instilled in us wasn't conducive to loving ourselves without shame and guilt. The fear and scarcity of our parent's generation framed their belief that love is not something you give away lightly. In their eyes, the only way to be fulfilled was to sacrifice, which meant that abandonment was part of our passage into adulthood and necessary for success.

In better understanding how we were raised to be people pleasers, we shouldn't overlook the devastating impact two destructive world-wars and a crippling depression had on how our parent's raised us. These heart-wrenching experiences caused our parents to harbor a healthy distrust for showing emotions, especially prolonged periods of happiness. And to be openly vulnerable was a sure sign of weakness and could put our well-being at risk in the adult world. Although we did our best to enjoy life to the fullest, we were always reminded that whatever we achieved, it was never good enough or that it could be taken from us. We were made to believe we were failures even if we succeeded. The only way to survive in this cold, harsh world was to lower our standards of self-worth, which the media, advertising and entertainment industries were all too eager to help us with.

It's easy to say that shame and guilt and feelings of abandonment were infused into our way of thinking by our parents and amplified by the many outside influences of society. At some point, however, it is up to each of us to take full responsibility for how we have lived our lives, then and now. There is no one else to please. At this stage we owe it to ourselves to clear out the regrets of the past and give ourselves the space to accept we did our best within the scope of what we knew.

Along with so many in my generation, I spent the better part of my life apologizing for who I am and convinced I didn't fit in because I was not good enough. The phrase, "I came into this world to be myself, for that I came", helps remind me that I am good enough just the way I am. It gives me permission to own my space and accept I am entitled to be myself without carrying shame or guilt for believing I didn't do enough to please others or live up to the expectations of what someone had of me.

*I AM MY OWN PRINCE CHARMING*

The outside world we once looked to for Prince Charming took on many forms. This ranged from our physical appearance, money and relationships to career accomplishments and the accumulation of materialistic items of all kinds. Many of us achieved one or more of these wants, but still found ourselves seeking for something more. The sacrifices we made to achieve our wants seemed to deliver more guilt and shame than happiness. This led nearly all Baby Boomers to ask themselves what is the meaning of life and what will it ever take to be fulfilled.

Who and what we are has been so blurred between nostalgic fantasy and misleading myths about love, success and aging, that the beautiful reality of our current lives seem to be in some strange holding pattern. A great many of our generation are living through the rosy hue reflection of the past, seemingly unaware of how good we have it now. This is a direct result of how we were raised through a scarcity driven mindset. Believing there is not enough to sustain our happiness in the present we are constantly seeking fulfillment everywhere but where we are.

As difficult as it will be for many of us to look upon the realities of our lives when laid bare and raw our collective story will reveal we are more than just statistically the largest segment of today's aging population or the demographic with the most disposable money. We're a

*Believing there is a void in our lives distorts the image we see of ourselves in the mirror, producing inner turmoil we think is caused by something outside of our control.*

generation in search of rediscovering the innocence that was stripped from us all those years ago. But what if our innocence was never lost and we have just been looking for it in all the wrong places?

Believing there is a void in our lives distorts the image we see of ourselves in the mirror, producing inner turmoil we think is caused by something outside of our control. If we are focused on a past no longer here, afraid to look into a future that is closer to not having us in it, it is easy to overlook our power to change how we interpret the reflection in the mirror of our present moment. Be it health, finances, romance or coping with the recent loss of a loved one, these challenges are part of our daily realities, but they are also rooted in scarcity. It's not to suggest that what we face today will all of a sudden disappear if we have a better understanding about the myth of scarcity. Our perceived challenges will be easier to manage though, when we uncover the root cause of why we believe we are lacking what we need to be fulfilled. The question is how do we gather the courage to remove the hunger of scarcity, forgive discriminatory beliefs of aging and undo our pain of abandonment, without getting tripped up in shame and guilt?

Not being aware of the difference between the truth of who we are and the myths we've been told about ourselves, is what holds in place the imaginary gap between fulfillment and despondency. So long as we keep this separation in place we may never fully come to appreciate what it means to love ourselves and enjoy the life we have right now. Gratefully, letting go of the belief that love is a mysterious idea hiding itself from us, and accepting age is not a cruel mistress that wounds us every time we look in the mirror, we begin to see the idea of Prince Charming we have sought after all these years is within us. Doing so removes the burden of seeking fulfillment in outside things and opens us up to living more fully in the present moment.

# Chapter 5

# ~ KNOW WHO YOU ARE ~

*"And the day came when the risk to remain tight in a bud*
*was more painful than the risk it took to blossom."*
*Anais Nin*

Larry Moss is a world-renowned acting coach and I am greatly honored to have studied with him for over six years. Larry believes, "that all actors – like all people – have a story to tell, although they are not always aware of it. When an actor has a tremendous success in a given piece of material, sometimes it parallels their own story in an emotional, psychological way." In fact, it was in his class that *My Blue Heaven* story was birthed as a story exercise. The story exercise that helped me bring this experience to life gives you a way of exploring your own life through a re-enactment of specific memories that you elevate into a performance. You must play each character in your story from their point of view. Thus, you must own their reason and rationale for the words and actions they take in your story. Each character requires you to master their voice, posture and gestures. This gives you a chance to walk in their shoes; to see their justification for their actions as they affect your story.

In Larry Moss's groundbreaking book, *The Intent to Live: Achieving Your True Potential as an Actor,* he states that, "Every play, novel, and screenplay has themes, and every human being's life has particular themes. Your theme can be surviving parental abuse and finding a way to live life fully and positively; it can be about struggle to resolve the loss of a loved one or the loss of a beloved place; surviving racial or sexual prejudice or a personal spiritual crisis; overcoming poverty or an oppressive government; overcoming too great a sense of entitlement or your own shame or guilt."

The importance of acting and the lessons I learned under Larry's inspiring, but emotionally grueling tutelage, helped me look at my own upbringing and prepared me to explore the collective experience of Baby Boomers through a different lens. Actors need to be seen, heard and understood. For most Boomers, this seldom happened in our childhood homes. We were not allowed to speak our truths, our voice was stifled and being ourselves was rarely tolerated. As a result, most of us didn't even know who our true, authentic selves were.

What does an unhappy childhood have to do with acting or any creative endeavor? In gifted and resilient individuals, stress and unhappiness in youth may help them to develop the power of fantasy and imagination. My generation helped change the world through our creativity and ingenuity. But, what if we had been allowed to express ourselves more openly at a younger age? What if we were raised with less stigma about being unique? And instead of being shamed for our differences, can we imagine how much we could have achieved had we been taught to see beauty in the unique ways we express ourselves? Would the world be different if the Baby Boomer generation were provided a nurturing space and stimulating framework to actually explore who we were without being shoved into a cookie-cutter mold?

We certainly cannot go back in time and change how we were raised and most of us wouldn't, even if we had the chance to. What's important in addressing these questions is to see where our lives could have been vastly improved and take that knowledge and pass it on to the younger generations. In doing so we help play a significant role in breaking the cycle of the Baby Boomer myths, which we have all unknowingly helped sustain.

Our struggles were not in vain. They helped us grow into who we are in ways that may not have happened if things were different during our childhood and early adult lives. Even so, what we cannot change about the past, we can change about our present lives right now.

> *Acting is living truthfully under imaginary circumstances. But what happens when we lose touch with the emotional truth of what is occurring in this moment?*

Within each of us is the creative power to clear whatever baggage we are still carrying and step into the roles we were born to play. However, to do that we have to give ourselves the space to not only be present, but it is necessary we learn to take responsibility for who we choose to be.

## ACT IT, WATCH IT OR CRITIQUE IT

When it comes to your performance as an actor, you can act it, watch it *(i.e. watch yourself)*, or critique it. You cannot do all three at the same time in the moment that you are creating the performance. Each facet requires you to be fully present. This is why I like to do live theatre. Live theatre provides a feeling of great joy! While performing for an audience, the atmosphere is charged with excitement and possible danger.

It is akin to being a flying acrobat performing a dangerous routine without the protection of a safety net. There are no second takes or second chances. Missed lines and mistakes on stage must be dealt with in the moment they happen, without any help from backstage. It is just you reacting, as your character would, to what has just happened. Acting is living truthfully under imaginary circumstances. But what happens when we lose touch with the emotional truth of what is occurring in this moment?

On Broadway, a famous actor playing Stanley in *"A Streetcar Named Desire"* lost his audience when the door to the apartment wouldn't open. Rather than explore an option that would have been emotionally relevant to the scene and character, he walked around and came in through the invisible wall. This completely took the audience out of the imaginary circumstances of the play. Later the actor said he regretted his action, realizing that his character Stanley, would have busted down the door with the stubborn knob, entered the room and continued the scene.

You can feel when the audience is with you and when they're not. When they are in the moment with you, you soar as a performer as you let go of the strain or anxiety of saying the lines "right". The magic is connecting with the emotions triggered by the words and stepping into the life you create for your character. It's about letting go and immersing yourself with her way of "being and living" on stage.

An actor that is in the moment is aware of being vulnerable to the power and emotion the spoken script evokes when you truly listen to the words and not just hear them. This allows you to feel the emotion of the moment itself. If you listen, the audience will listen. If you see what you are describing to the audience, they will see it too. This only happens when you are in the present moment. And it directly applies to real life. Being present and allowing one's self to flow, without being worried about the critique of someone else, most prominently your own inner critic, is not something most Baby Boomers were raised to be well versed in. The majority of us were not raised to truly know who we are.

## THE CHOICE

An actor's talent is in their choices. These range from how the costume is worn, to how the lines are spoken, the choice of the props and how they are used to convey the life of their character. Each choice is directly aligned with every movement and word spoken by an actor, which carries a specific relationship to every person, place, object and event that is part of the lines being delivered. Because of their choices, a well-prepared actor enters the scene knowing where they just came from and what they want to accomplish in the scene.

As an actor, our highest purpose is to be the emotional conduit for the audience. Actors allow themselves to be the catalyst, so that the audience has permission to feel their feelings by experiencing their own emotional reactions. The

> *When we stopped making choices that felt good to us and instead made choices based on how others would perceive us, we lost touch with the one person that matters most in our life, our own selves.*

more the actor is in touch with her character's feelings, the more the audience is going to be invited to explore their own. We can draw the correlation of how we make choices to fit within society's beliefs, to an actor's choice to suspend all form of doubt and be present in creating a reality where they and their audience can tap into a higher realm of self-awareness. If an actor's choices can impact the audience's emotions by their total immersion into the moment, is it not also true that when we, as individuals, make the choice to be present with our feelings, we are inviting society and all those we interact with to do the same?

We were raised to perform our lives according to a strict set of rules, myths and beliefs that either accentuated our gifts to a pre-determined level, or circumvented them altogether. Either way, when we stopped making choices that felt good to us and instead made choices based on how others would perceive us, we lost touch with the one person that matters most in our life, our own selves.

The Oscar season always reminds me of an acting truth: great performances flow from the actor's ability to recognize, accept and use all facets of their personality that formerly would be rejected, resisted and hidden from view. From their uncensored, inner creative core that embraces all parts of themselves, their work is filled with more aliveness and vibrant expression. This can absolutely be applied in our daily lives and we do not have to be Oscar winning actors to achieve this.

Let us use this moment of our lives to make a choice to look into our soul and call forth all the unlovable, shunned parts of ourselves with honor and gratitude. Ask each part what is the value and service it provides us. Be still and listen in this opened, uncritical space for the unloved part of you to speak its truth. It will reveal how it serves you. From there you can take that lesson and apply it to your life, which invites others to do the same for themselves. As Helen Keller shared with the world, "Everything has its wonders, even darkness and silence, and I learn whatever state I may be in, therein to be content."

## *MY VISIT WITH ZENYATTA*

When the legendary horse, Zenyatta, won The 2010 Horse of the Year Award, her owner, Jerry Moss, read the following poem by Pricilla Clark during his Eclipse Awards speech.

"If you love thoroughbred horses, you go through life hoping that you can see just one more in whose presence the clouds fall away to reveal the mountaintop. It can take a generation or infinitely longer for such a horse to arrive, a horse that is capable of carrying the human heart. For the last one hundred years we know them all by name, but Zenyatta brought to us a beauty that was a tonic for the soul. She allowed us to believe in the impossible, and it was the light of her being as much as the thrill of her races that got us dancing. Zenyatta was transformative."

For my 2010 birthday wish, I wanted to meet Zenyatta, this world famous racehorse. She had already won 19 straight races and she was now preparing for her 20th and final race. Being an actor, I never thought of

> *"What is it with you humans, you make everything so complicated? Why wouldn't I win every race? This is who I am and this is what I do."*
>
> *Zenyatta*

celebrities as being any better than my lesser known but equally talented, fellow creative professionals. But Zenyatta was different. There was something about her that transcended not only her species but also the profession by which she had established a second-to-none legacy. I had to meet her.

Through a group of close friends I knew from the racing world, a visit with Zenyatta was arranged. In the early morning we arrived at Zenyatta's barn. She was in her stall with her head out, awaiting her trainer, John Shireffs, to start her morning workout routine. I walked over to her. Here was

Zenyatta, one of the largest and most physically imposing horses to ever race, looking down at me. Without even thinking whether she would understand, I said to her, "Zenyatta, I have always wanted to meet you and I am so excited to be here with you." She liked this, and I had her full attention now.

Her magnificent presence, with the regal tilt to her head and brilliant attentive gaze, was focused on my face. Zenyatta's truth is simple and her gifts are readily seen and experienced. But there is more there than just what our eyes can see. And I felt this connection between us in an undeniable way.

I continued with an equal dose of enthusiasm and genuine gratitude, "Zenyatta, I want to ask you a question. I am an actor and I would psych myself out long before I ever booked 19 jobs in a row. How did you win 19 consecutive races?" The mood shifted between us. She looked at me with bemused disdain and said, "What is it with you humans, you make everything so complicated? Why wouldn't I win every race? This is who I am and this is what I do."

I know it seems hard to believe, but Zenyatta did look into my face and say this. I could never make something like that up. And the way she communicated to me isn't even how I think or speak. Let's be clear, I'm no horse whisperer. And, Zenyatta did not open her mouth and speak as you or I would. It was a language of the mind, of the heart. Some describe it as a form of telepathy. It is when you tap into the thought waves of another living being and intuitively connect on a level that words could never aptly describe. I'd never had an experience like that, nor have I had one since then. The experience irrevocably and positively change my life for the better.

Yes, Zenyatta is a race horse, I am an actor and these are our gifts. But what is a gift if it is not unconditionally accepted? And how can we accept our gifts if we are not accepting of who we are? No drama, no doubts, no interference, just pure acceptance of our gift and knowing who we are. This is what struck me about Zenyatta. There was no doubt or overthinking in anything she did. It was with a sense of uncompromising purpose, present minded ownership of the moment and pure confidence.

Once you own your gift in this manner you can give it away for others to enjoy without a sense of guilt, or an unrealistic set of demands for what we get in return. It is in this complete trust of our purpose that we have removed any lingering and debilitating thoughts of unworthiness. Nothing can derail us but our own limiting ideas about who we are and what we are here to do. And what can be limited in our gifts if we take complete ownership in knowing who we are, which is a full acceptance of our gifts?

On that day I met Zenyatta, it was this level of ownership of who and what we are that she revealed to me in a way I'd never before considered. So now, before I go in to an audition, rehearsal, performance or film shoot, I say to myself, "I am here to share my gifts and contribute to the project's vision. This is who I am and this is what I do."

Thank you, Zenyatta, for this most wonderful of life's lessons.

*ACCEPT WHO I AM*

Great acting looks simple and effortless. It is neither of those things. Auditions for me were all about being the little girl again, waiting to be asked and chosen. This was harkening back to those days of being groomed to be the one chosen by Prince Charming, which either validated my worthiness or lack thereof. If I were not fully aware of who I am and accepting of my gifts, those auditions are torturous because

I place my self-worth in someone else's hands other than my own.

Acting teachers, directors and Zenyatta have taught me to own my talent with confidence and accept myself just the way I am. Now, I enter audition rooms and step onto stages and sets with confidence and joy. I am here to offer my talent and enhance the vision of the project. I am acceptable and lovable just as I am. Who I am is enough. I don't have to overact or overdo anything to prove I am worthy of being valued and picked for the roles.

Actors don't make the choice of who gets cast. The final choices are outside of our control. But as Zenyatta taught me, I am an actor and this is who I am and what I do. Any attempt to be in command of that which is beyond my control, is a clear sign I am not fully aware of who I am, or what I am there in the moment to do. When this happens for any of us, we're attempting to be someone we're not by controlling the uncontrollable. This creates unnecessary strain. And who needs that?

During my years training to be an actor, I started to see in myself many of the limiting beliefs I'd been aware of, but rarely, if ever, took time to closely examine. As an actor we are required to be present with our emotions, but this was not how I was raised, or for that matter, how most Baby Boomers were raised. In an era of self-preservation and a belief in the idea of survival, no one had time to be present with their emotions.

The story we were told was the less vulnerable we believed we were, the more inner drive we had to survive and succeed. We had very few options to explore who we were because our roles as women and men were pre-set and we were told to fit within those roles or suffer the consequences. It's still that way for most people, regardless of age. This is changing at a rapid pace as we are living in a more transparent world. More than ever before, people are choosing to know who they are and express this vulnerability in ways that were once frowned upon.

## SHIFTING PERCEPTIONS OF LIFE

During the middle part of my life I came to see that my life path was narrowing as my awareness of the path itself was widening. At the time, I felt this was isolated to just me. As I reached a later stage of life and the character of McGranny and the *Drive-Thru, Make It Your Own®* campaign came into existence, I started to see that my path was more similar to other Baby Boomers than I had previously imagined. The details of our lives were different, but the overarching emotional experiences of our world and how much baggage we were carrying from our early upbringing, was remarkably similar.

To finally see I was not alone helped me liberate myself from feeling as if I had done something wrong. Everyone deals with their shifting perceptions of life differently, even if the underlining premise to live a fulfilling life is the same. For me, I began adapting acting principles to the workings of my everyday life and creating a brighter, more shining, vibrant version of what I had tried so hard to achieve in my earlier days.

If there is a contrast between myself and other Baby Boomers, it is here at this pivotal point, the magical number of 55. When many Baby Boomers were eyeing the finish line of achievements and contemplating retirement in their mid-to-late fifties, I was starting to get clear on what I wanted my life to look like. It was time to reclaim the enchantment and charming life of "My Blue Heaven"; a life I thought I had lost when paradise and my innocence slipped away. So, I went back to many of the questions I learned in acting school, such as:

- What do I want?

- What do I want to accomplish?

- What do I have to do in order to live my "Life Charming"?

- What are the obstacles between me and my "Life Charming"?

Other transferable skills that I have applied in my daily life from my experience as an actor included:

- Know who you are

- Know what you are listening for

- Know what you are risking

- Know what you want to accomplish in "this scene"

- Know what motivates you to speak

It was quite clear to me that my creative experiences as an actor were easily transferable to everyday living. These experiences and the framework of the questions that prepared me for acting scenes would later become the basis for the *Drive-Thru, Make It Your Own*® campaign as well as this book. So how do these apply to undoing the myth of Prince Charming? Let's take a look at where and how that myth got started and how it has grown over the last 50 to 60 years.

# Chapter 6

## ~ WHERE IS MY PRINCE CHARMING? ~

*"Love isn't something you find. Love is something that finds you."*
*Loretta Young*

Prince Charming lives in my heart. My mother's voice planted him there while reading all those enchanting stories that start with, "Once upon a time, a long time ago" and ending with "they lived happily ever after." In every story, Prince Charming always saved the girl of his choice and the girl got the man of her dreams. For millions of other little girls and boys who grew up during the Baby Boomer era those fantastic tales, usually told through Golden Books, not only formed our childhood beliefs but they helped raise us to learn our roles in society.

The girls would be taught the Three P's. Be prim, proper and patient, even as we anxiously waited for that magical moment when Prince Charming would choose us as the woman of his dreams. The boys were taught their own set of rules; each one rigidly underscored by the idea that they are the Knight In Shining Armor. The visuals of lifting his chosen girl onto his white steed and galloping off to create a new and wonderful life seemed less like a fantasy than it was an expectation that had to be met. This painted the image of women as the damsel in distress and that we were incomplete until we were saved by Prince Charming.

> *The idea of who we are is projected onto the screen of our lives, which reflects back to us how we think of ourselves.*

The endings of the Golden Book fairytales helped underscore unrealistic standards and expectations set by our families and society. If we did not fit into society's approved roles, we were told a "happily ever after" life was out of our grasp. To us, Prince Charming was the reward for obeying the rules of our parents and following the path that society's myths had laid out as our pre-destined future.

The blueprint of these mythical stories set up an entire generation to be unfulfilled by the realities of the world we were groomed for. When our expectations were not met, and they usually were not, the arrows of rejection tore into our hearts. Each time this happened it accentuated the emotional trauma from the abandonment issues we all went through in one way or another when we were children. The desire to fill this void put us on a course to chase after love through whatever means we felt we could be fulfilled. This is where Prince Charming took on the symbolic role of anything or anyone that we saw outside of ourselves whom we believed would bring us happiness and make us feel loved.

## WORTHY OF LOVE

The idea of who we are is projected onto the screen of our lives, which reflects back to us how we think of ourselves. If we are to live a life worthy of who we are, it is necessary to recognize that our worthiness is not given to us through the approval of someone we are in a relationship with or in the accumulation of any materialistic items we pursue. Who we are must first be accepted from within otherwise we will confuse our self-worth with what we see as our external projections.

It is easy for the idea of Prince Charming to be mistaken as a romantic symbol, but it is far more than that. When we accept that we are worthy of love, only then will we be aware of the abundance and wholeness shining out from us that attracts and draws to us all that we desire and deserve. Sending out mixed signals as to what we love and do not love about ourselves is a recipe for attracting a projection of ourselves we do not like. This is why scarcity is not isolated to one experience or a single belief, but to all things we draw into our awareness.

Even if we find joy in a relationship, or happiness in something we buy, it is temporary. This is expected as a normal course of life. It's not uncommon for us to feel betrayed when the people and things upon which we placed our hopes and dreams turn out to be less than what we wanted. Soon, what we longed for will not satisfy our need to be happy, leaving us further disillusioned about our self-worth. To adjust our focus inward is to let go of a long-held belief in the myth that happiness and love are limited and can be found outside of us. This requires us to let go of believing there is a symbolic idea of Prince Charming out there that can make us whole.

*Being grateful for what we have reduces the longing for something better and diminishes the fear that our happiness can be taken away.*

The idea of us lacking anything is rooted in how we have defined our experience in the past and then applied it to the future. In the process of projecting an idea of time that no

90

longer exists to a moment in time that has yet to happen we ignore the beautiful realities of the present moment. If we jump over the present moment, there is the feeling that there is no ground underneath us, which keeps us trying to reach what is ultimately an unreachable goal. Once we see our lives in the present moment it becomes a lot easier to enjoy what we have now.

Being grateful for our experiences and what we have in our life right now reduces the longing for something better and diminishes the fear that our happiness can be taken away. This may sound like an oversimplification to some people. But the disparity between what we are grateful for and what we lament is at the heart of why it is so important to understand and ultimately free ourselves from the myths we grew up on.

## BEGGARS CAN'T BE CHOOSERS

The majority of Baby Boomers were brought up to believe our lives were successful if we fit within the narrow categories society deemed worthy of us. This was especially true for millions of women who were not chosen by their ideal Prince Charming and instead were told to lower their standards because "beggars can't be choosers." Women were not the only ones from our generation who were taught to lower their expectations. Men were raised to believe that to be accepted and worthy of society's accolades, they had to adhere to the strict rules of being the all-accomplishing Prince Charming.

But, if men did not like how society's standards were being applied to them, they had more leeway than women to change the course of their lives and break free of the myths. There was an ugly double standard applied to those who defied society's guidelines for Prince Charming. Men who succeeded in breaking through the limits of myths were often labeled as "trailblazers" or "overachievers". For women who attempted such a thing, they were given much less room to explore their gifts. And the names given to those women who attempted to "overachieve" were anything but respectful.

Despite the double standard for women and men, having opportunities to succeed taken from us reinforced the myth that there isn't enough love, money and happiness to go around. This also set up the need to seek fulfillment in external activities that were not necessarily in our best interest. Here is where the idea of seeking our Prince Charming takes a rather dark turn.

Seeking alternative means to feel loved and acknowledged, millions of Baby Boomers wound up in toxic relationships, unsatisfying jobs and dysfunctional lifestyles they hoped would bring them happiness and fulfillment, only to end up harboring deep resentment for having settled for something less than ideal. The gap between what many would call "the haves and have not's" widened during the Baby Boomer years. Instead of feeling the freedom to choose our destiny, many of us were forced into situations where we became the beggars, hoping we'd be noticed and chosen by the right man, woman or company. It seemed that no matter what we did, or how much we succeeded, we all went begging for acknowledgment and love. Fearing our opportunities for acceptance were limited, most of us grabbed what opportunities we could, settling for less than what we wanted and deserved.

Stuck in a world of mediocrity, the disparity between what many desired and what they believed they were capable of having, seemed to reinforce the truth of the Baby Boomer myths as being unchangeable. No matter where any of us fell within the spectrum of society's standards, the process of being groomed to accept our roles and the consequences if we tried to change them permeated the entire social structure. So, while our ideas of what symbolized Prince

Charming may have been different for each of us, the framework and overall experience of looking for our Prince Charming was the same.

*TAKING FULL RESPONSIBILITY*

At this stage of our lives, many Boomers I have spoken with consider themselves worthy of love and confess they gave up on the idea of Prince Charming long ago. This may be true for some, but it's important to not lose sight on how the myths of Baby Boomers appear resolved in one area of our life, while hiding themselves in others, often disguised as issues outside of our control to change. Just when we think one myth is solved, another one creeps up on us without realizing we simply ignored the root cause of all the myths, which is our belief in scarcity. This can be explored in a number of areas but one that is quite overt is how we continuously buy into threats the media delivers about our dwindling sense of happiness and safety as we age.

Baby Boomers are the generation that helped give rise to the self-improvement industry, but we also helped fuel the negativity that permeates the message put forth by the media, advertisement and entertainment industries. Just because we have more access to stories and imageries of the world does not mean the perceived threats we encounter today are different than the ones we faced when we were young and naïve. The difference is that now we are older, we have a better frame of reference for what is real and what isn't – or do we?

> *"We cannot solve our problems with the same thinking we used when we created them."*
>
> *Albert Einstein*

To fully understand the power of scarcity is to see that the idea is nothing more than the denial of responsibility for our own sense of happiness. If we believe someone or something can take away our joy, than we have temporarily given up our power to love who we are because we are constantly at the mercy of others defining our self-worth. As children, we were at the mercy of adults. But as adults, it would seem we have much more control over our lives. If this is true how come there remains a pervasive belief that our safety and happiness is at the mercy of other people's thoughts and actions?

As an example, society's belief on aging is that the older we get, the less control of our lives we have. This may be true for those who are faced with extreme health issues, but for most Baby Boomers we are healthier, wealthier and happier today than many of our parents were when they were our age. Even so, the media, advertisement and entertainment industries are still hawking outdated beliefs about aging that many in society accept as an unchangeable truth. It is up to us to take responsibility for our lives and not allow our self-worth or happiness to be influenced by shame and blame campaigns that have little to nothing to do with our past, present or future.

*THE PATH TO OUR FUTURE*

There is no magical thinking that will suddenly alter our future, or improve our present state of mind, if we continue to think that life is outside of our control to change. The step we take right now on the path of our best life leads us directly to our future. The intention of that step is what determines the experience of the future, and the future occurs in the moment the step is taken. Only by changing the direction of that first step, which is to change one's intention, will the path itself change and with it, our future.

Reuniting with our inner Prince Charming becomes much easier when we let go of how we allowed the myths to determine the way we saw ourselves in the past. If we continue placing the same meaning on our lives as we once did, the intent we apply to carrying out our thoughts in the present and future stays the same. We never escape our past by doing this. As Albert Einstein famously said, "We cannot solve our problems with the same thinking we used when we created them."

Responsibility for our happiness is about real change, not some motivational shower that temporarily washes away a bad day, only to have that day show up again and again. The path to the future we desire starts within, which is where we release our attachment to outside gratification and bring forth our inner Prince Charming. But first, we have to understand how we got it all backwards and gave away our power to determine our self-worth in a world of escapism.

No generation is immune to abandonment issues, but few have dealt with it in the ways and means Baby Boomers have. We were the first generation that lived in what many refer to as the Golden Age of America. After World War II there was a global sigh of relief that peace was achieved as optimism filled the lungs of our parents and grandparents. But, our parents had little time to rejoice as the threat of Communism, nuclear war and the cost of living became an everyday challenge. Enter the age of escapism.

To offset the doom and gloom realities the media was feeding society, entertainment and consumerism grew beyond our wildest imaginations. Unlike any generation before us, the media, advertisement and entertainment industries were giving us a glimpse into new worlds, many of which we were now longing to be a part of. Fairytale stories of living the American dream, told in a myriad of different formats, helped serve as a form of escapism for many in our generation. But the roles young women and men of our era were being groomed for were a harsh reminder that there weren't enough opportunities for all of us. Even so, this new age of escapism fueled our optimism for a better life with what appeared to be choices for when, where and how to fill the void we all felt but had little to no understanding of the consequences of these choices.

*BEING GOOD ENOUGH*

For me, and many others I grew up with, it wasn't so much that we were driven by a desire to achieve a life-long dream or change the world as much as it was gaining some sense of approval from our parents. We just wanted to know we were good enough. Having to compete with others for opportunities and approval of our self-worth drove us to create new ways to escape what was becoming an unbearable amount of stress. The degree of stress that compounded as the years wore on gave rise to many industries, including but not limited to; divorce attorneys, marriage counselors, psychiatrists, health and wellness products, cosmetic surgeries and a host of high-end luxury items, all designed to either fix or distract us from the reality of our lives. The closer Prince Charming seemed to be, the further away we got from loving who we are.

Whether it was a relationship with another person, a service or product, the ultimate symbol of Prince Charming represented being good enough. Looking back on my life it is clear to me now that the first and most prevalent form Prince Charming took was my mother. My mother's illness profoundly shaped how I saw my relationship with the world. Feeling abandoned at the tender age of five, as I got older I was determined to fill the void of abandonment by proving my worthiness to her. Based on the research I've conducted for this book, in addition to the numbers of Boomers I've spoken with over the years, it is clear that I am not alone in this feeling, even if our life scripts and the details of what we have experienced are different.

For me, the way I measured my self-worth was through the attention and acknowledgment of my mother. This carried over to how I was perceived as a student in high school and college, to being a good wife, respected business owner and actor. I was driven to fill the

*Whether it was a relationship with another person, a service or product, the ultimate symbol of Prince Charming represented being good enough.*

categories by which I was being judged as successful or not. This all led back to how my mother would see me based on my accomplishments. What I wanted to achieve, however, could never fulfill me because I was confused as to the true source of where my fulfillment originated.

I was not aware at the time that everything I was chasing after was me giving away my own inner power to be happy.

Without being aware of this, I was destined to chase for love and worthiness outside of myself, as were tens of millions of other Baby Boomers. For all the escapism that helped us create a new and exciting world for ourselves, we still had to face what we were originally escaping from in the first place, ourselves.

## RECLAIMING PARADISE

For a brief moment in time, our lives seemed like paradise. Our generation appeared to have it all. And then, what felt like a dream turned into a nightmare for many. The original moment we lost paradise wasn't necessarily during adulthood, but during childhood. This marked the loss of our innocence. For each of us this happened differently. My mother's illness changed her life and in turn, it changed mine. I could surmise that I never had a choice or a chance to do anything about it. But I did.

The path to navigate my way back to my own inner Prince Charming has been as difficult as it is liberating. First I had to sort through the legacy of my parents, especially my mother's incessant messages about what it meant to be an obedient girl and how to fit into society's closed-minded ideas about women. The myth that being the ideal loving daughter would earn me the perfect life was not at all what I imagined it to be. The more success I enjoyed the more disappointment I experienced. This added to the disillusionment about my self-worth and reinforced the myth there isn't enough happiness to go around.

As my mother and I would age, and our relationship would ebb and flow over time, we were again faced with a life altering experience as her progressing dementia and other ailments would accelerate the shift in her health. Here I was a fully-grown adult and again I am feeling like that five year old and my entire world was crumbling. It felt like I was losing paradise with my mother's downward spiral, but it was actually a reoccurring experience whose origins dated back to when I was five years old. That is when I first learned how to live in this world without my mother shining the sunlight on my face.

Unlike those formative years as a little girl, where surviving meant trying to make sense of things that made absolutely no sense, as an adult I had accumulated the skills and knowledge to navigate turbulent experiences and understand them. Like most Baby Boomers, I became a master at coping with change. But coping with change is not the same as taking responsibility for one's own sense of happiness.

To hide from the obvious truth of our inner strength means we will continue to seek for acceptance outside of ourselves, as we were taught how to survive this way. This makes us highly susceptible to buying into the depressing doom-and-gloom stories the world spins about aging, love, health and money. To unbind ourselves from these mythical and scarcity driven stories is to truly open the floodgates of abundance that washes away the stain of shaming and blaming ourselves for thinking we are not enough.

## ACCEPTING WHO AND WHERE WE ARE

We live our lives with complicated and conflicting operating systems, each of them protected by a dense layer of contradicting beliefs that keep us shackled to the status quo. An example of this is how we chase results we fear achieving, while at the same time we fear the consequences of what would happen if we don't achieve the results we chase.

For many people, their beliefs are tied to a belief they are not worthy of achieving what they desire. For others, there is the fear that if they achieve their life long goals, they will be burdened by new and overwhelming responsibilities, so they hold back and pretend to be content with mediocrity. And then, there are those who are driven to achieve their goals to prove they are better than others, but are never satisfied with what they achieve, so there is little to no joy in their lives despite the massive level of success they have. All of this is framed within the myth of scarcity and the myth there isn't enough happiness to go around.

*What are we willing to do to have what we think will make us happier? And perhaps most important, is what will any of this do for us when and if we achieve it?*

The ever present threat of loss, whether we get what we want or not, overshadows our accomplishments, driving even the most successful Baby Boomers to seek all sorts of methods for protecting what they thought could be taken from them. This isn't happiness, nor is it accepting that we are our own Prince Charming. This is a nightmare that never ends, for everywhere we look there is the perception of a threat to our well-being.

This brings us full circle with the myth of Prince Charming and how our need to seek fulfillment outside of us encompasses every facet of our lives. The symbolic imagery we have of Prince Charming is the Knight In Shining Armor arriving in the form of anything we desire. But what is it that we truly desire? A facelift to make us prettier? A new home or car to make us look successful? A new relationship to help us feel more loved? More money to help us feel confident and secure? What are we willing to do to have what we think will make us happier? And perhaps most important, what will any of this do for us when and if we achieve it?

The list of things we believe are going to complete us and provide us a happy, fulfilled life is endless. And just when we think we have this all figured out, life rounds the corner of our slumbering thoughts of grandeur and literally smacks us upside our overly anxious, self-indulged noggin. All that we once held so dear and all the things we sought to make our lives better, cease to matter when the inescapable presence of death is knocking on our door.

What is after death is clearly open for debate, but what is indisputable is that our bodies and the experiences we have in them will one day cease to exist. This takes us right back to the myth of scarcity that says happiness is fleeting and cannot last. So how do we release the pain of believing we will never be good enough, if what we think we're good enough for won't last? Such is the quandary of facing the inevitable conclusion that everything in life will ultimately come to an end, including our search for Prince Charming. Herein lies both the source of our pain, as much as it is the release from it.

When the end of our life appears on the horizon, or we are faced with the death of someone we love, all the myths seem to rise up at once to protect us. We lean on them, each myth seemingly serving as a version of our Prince Charming. Appearing as our best friend, and believing that we will be protected from being abandoned and hurt, the myths and their teachings can easily serve as a crutch to get us through what seems to be impossible to deal with situations. By letting go of our fear of death we release the false sense of security the seven myths provide and open ourselves up to a new way of living. For, if we refuse to accept the power to be at peace with ourselves is from within, the painful experience of abandonment, which is personified in the idea of death, will be impossible for us to handle.

# Chapter 7

# ~ THERE'S A LOT OF PAIN
# IN THIS FILE ~

*"Nature is resilient and so must we be."*
*Joanie Marx*

It is a warm sunny day as I skip beside by mother in our front yard. I am four years old and this is one of my earliest memories. We have matching blue watering cans, only mine is much smaller than hers. The rose bushes, which beautifully line the concrete patio, are our destination. We reach my favorite white rose bush and my mother and I give it a drink of water. A group of yellow butterflies, who have been silently sitting between the leaves and thorns of the rose bush, are startled by our laughing and splashing water. The butterflies quickly emerge from their hiding spot, forming a yellow cloud above the bushes.

My eyes are transfixed on them and I follow their movement with amazement. I extend my hand outward in the hopes that maybe I can play with them. One of the butterflies breaks from the group and circles back, landing softly on my outstretched hand. A mixture of momentary shock is washed away by wonder and joy that now shines forth from my face. The butterfly wants to be my friend and I am elated!

My mother remains a few feet away, busy pruning and watering; unaware of this enchanting moment I am experiencing. Mindful not to startle her, I slowly engage my new friend; gently touching her wings as she rhythmically opens and closes them. Picking her up, I now hold both wings together, so we can have a secret eye-to-eye conversation. She tells me the magical experiences of being a butterfly and how much she loves my white rose bush. Cupping my newfound friend between my hands, I can feel her jump up and down with excitement as I skip around the yard showing her my special hiding places. When I release my hold to bid my butterfly friend goodbye, I am taken aback. Instead of flying away, she lays motionless in my hand.

My mother can make everything fine and I run to her, exclaiming, "Make the butterfly fly." She takes one look at the lifeless butterfly in my palm and calmly says, "I can't, Joan." I am undeterred and in a louder voice I say again, "Make the butterfly fly!"

"Joan, I can't make the butterfly fly. It's dead." In a more insistent tone, I refuse to give in, "You can Mommy! You can make it fly! It's not dead." My mother can see I am refusing to accept the death of the butterfly. "I'm sorry, Joan. But there's nothing I can do."

With anger like none I had known before I emphatically declare, "She is a perfectly good butterfly. Now, you make her fly!" My mother again replies, "I can't make the butterfly fly." Seething with rage that is beginning to mix in with a rising despair of sadness, I stand with my outstretched hand glaring at my mother. None of this makes any sense. I can't understand how the butterfly stopped moving or why my mother won't help. Finally, I put my hand down and the butterfly slides to the concrete, but she doesn't feel the fall. Hugging my little blue watering can to my chest, I defiantly walk away from my mother.

As I grow up, I come to realize the impact this seemingly inconsequential event has on my life. Within me is a fierce determination to make all events and people meet my expectations. Throughout my life I gain a reputation with friends and colleagues that I will work against all odds to manifest the desired outcome that harmonically synchs up with my wants. This is a trait that is both admired and one that intimidates many.

What no one knew, until now, is that when I find myself trapped in a situation that is untenable, and beyond all help, I will silently utter the code phrase to myself for walking away, which is, "Make the butterfly fly." This reminds me of letting go of something that cannot work, no matter how much I want it to. Little did I fathom that my first conscious encounter with death all those years ago would circle back around and beckon me to face the reality of using these words for my mother's own life, and ultimately my own.

## IT FELT LIKE THE END

My mother lived in the same house I had been raised in. This is where she and I both knew she wanted to be until she passed on. In the beginning stages of her downward spiral, it was me calling her on the phone countless times a day to cue her to get-up, eat, shower and care for her dog. After endless conversations with my mother where she would tell me "tomorrow I'll get up early and be fine" which never happened, I moved onto the next phase. I hired a lovely lady to come and wake her as well as prepare the meals.

110

Still later, I hired full time live-in help. Finally, no amount of coaching would get her to bathe, eat or not sleep the day away. Rounds and rounds of doctor appointments yielded the Multi-Infarct Dementia diagnosis. I could be with her round the clock and the second I went out the door, my mother had no memory of me ever being there. All my help and love could not change her situation and this was not an easy reality for me to accept. The undeniable shifts in her health and behavior, though, brought me to a very difficult realization. There was a real possibility she would have to be moved to a nursing home.

My determination to remain on course and honor my mother's wishes prompted a staunch refusal to give in. I believed that she would die if I took her out of her home. I kept ratcheting up the caregiving services

> *All my help and love could not change her situation and this was not an easy reality for me to accept.*

and bringing in more help to support her. Calls to self-help groups all gave the same advice. I must find a nursing home while she was still ambulatory or none would even take her. Then one night she fell out of bed.

111

I thought she had broken her hip. But the hospital x-rays showed she hadn't broken any bones. The revelation from this emergency  visit was more disturbing and far more challenging to grasp than if she had broken bones. The doctor on call that night carefully reviewed her medical file. When he was done, his eyes shifted to my mother and then they were trained on me. Very calmly he said, "There's a lot of pain in this medical file." I thought that was incredibly compassionate of him to say, but it also got me to think about my  mother's life and her philosophy with handling situations. Although I had my code phrase, "Make the butterfly fly," which I had used to gracefully exit situations that had no positive outcome, it become clear to me that in ways I hadn't considered before, I was very much like my mother when it came to sticking with things way beyond the point of any semblance of a positive outcome. But, I could not deny that my mother's health was beyond the point of no return.

My mother comes from what is often referred to as, "The Greatest Generation". They were raised to never give up, to keep on fighting in the face of extreme opposition, which is one primary reason World War II was won. This is a noble and honorable trait and one that I carry within me, as do millions of Boomers. But, there is a cruel irony to this. There will be critical moments in all of our lives where we are faced with walking away from a situation that does more harm than good to stay in it, despite all of our best intentions to manifest a favorable outcome. It may be years before the harmful effects take shape from not letting go, but there is no denying the evidence that we have all been adversely affected when we overstay our welcome in a situation. In my mother's state of health it was incredibly difficult to accept but I had to utter the words, "Make the butterfly fly."

There was no more second guessing about what needed to be done. The week she fell out of bed I moved my beloved mother to an assisted living nursing home. No longer could I or my team of caregivers guarantee her physical safety. Next time we might not be so lucky. As I carefully led her out of the home she'd been in for her entire adult life and into the car, I was emotionally struck by the realization my mother would never come back to her home. Nor would the hoped for miracle that my Mother Charming would come back to me.

*ROCKHAVEN*

Rockhaven was chosen as the nursing home for my mother. It specialized in caring for women with dementia. When we arrived the head nurse, a woman named Cassie, warmly greeted us. I introduced myself as "Matilda's mother." What a Freudian slip. Roles were reversed and this was still a work in progress for me to accept. This was like the moment when I went to college and for the first time I was away from my mother. Except in this scenario, I was dropping my mother off and it was the first time in decades she would be living under a new roof.

Rockkhaven was founded in 1920 as a sanitarium for women with Tuberculosis. With extensive grounds and mature Coastal Oak trees, it is nestled in a quiet foothill community. Marilyn Monroe's mother was treated there. In the 1960's the Sanitarium was changed into a home for women with dementia. The property was spread over three and a half acres and contained several small cottages with inviting covered porches. Only 50 women were cared for in this inviting "Bed and Breakfast" style facility. The women who lived here were grouped into different cottages bases on their mental acuity and mobility. The daily activities and all meals were served in a dining hall. Most ladies walked to the hall, which could easily be described as a parade of 1930's proper ladies, all well-coiffed, manicured and dressed in lovely clothes with pearls, carrying gloves and hand bags.

Social events and all holidays were celebrated with a beautiful cut glass punchbowl with pedestal handled punch glasses. The punch was made with ice cream and ginger ale. It tasted exactly like all the punches I had ever had at school dances and sorority parties. Being there and observing how well the women were cared for was akin to be being in a dream where everything was orchestrated, as you would have imagined a dream life would be.

Standing outside Rockhaven, Cassie asked my mother if she would like to have lunch and my mother agreed, but only on the condition there was dessert. Cassie said it was ice cream, which was my mother's favorite dessert. Cassie then reached out and gently took my mother's arm and together they walked into the home.

My mother didn't say goodbye to me. She didn't say thank you. Nor did she even look back in my direction. She and Cassie simply disappeared into her future. That was one of the toughest moments of my life. I remember silently crying out, "Daddy where are you when I need you? And dead is no excuse!" Then my mother's voice in my head repeated what she told me as a young girl, "Joan, you have to stick with things. When it comes to what you want, you cannot waver. Trust your instincts. All of it will work out in the end."

At this seminal moment in our lives, it felt like the end. That's because it was. But in this end there were new beginnings emerging, I just couldn't see them. Despite my emotional state on that day, I called upon my lessons learned in Larry Moss's acting classes about being present. I could not continue on in my life and make it a life worth living if I continued to hold to an idea of the past that was no longer relevant. Life had thrown me an ad-lib and I had little choice but to flow with it.

Many people, including myself, have been tripped up in these profound and often unexpected exchanges with life. I have found that a key ingredient for crossing the bridge from where we used to dwell to a new way of living is gratitude. Having gratitude for what led us to this point, opens doors that were previously closed, or that we had no idea were even there to begin with. Gratitude makes change easier and it allows us to gracefully go with the flow, which is the essence of being in the present moment.

## BE LIKE A WILLOW TREE

In Colonial America, the willow tree was a symbol of grief. Possibly because when we experience loss, we remember the "Weeping Willow", a resilient tree that grows on the banks of a stream. Like the willow, we grow by the river of our tears, learning how to live as we struggle through our losses. Surviving Colonial family members would memorialize their loved ones by embroidering samplers featuring the weeping willow, and the willow would appear on many gravestones from this period. Our ancestors understood that, like the willow, the wind of grief will move us forward.

*Gratitude makes change easier and it allows us to gracefully go with the flow, which is the essence of being in the present moment.*

The willow tree survives by bending to the wind's will instead of attempting to remain rigid and unmovable in the face of the force. The supple branches sway willingly to the wind's demands, thus saving itself from being broken, or ripped off. We can be more like the willow and give into the winds of change that blow with time's passage. We can accept that the wind sweeps away the landscape of our childhood. For many Baby Boomers, as it is for a lot of people, the longer we are here in this world the more we have to face life without all the beloved people and places we grew up with.

Too often, we allow ourselves to get caught up in the emotional trauma of grief that seems to be an integral part of change. Rather than face it, learn from it and then release it, we drag grief around with us like a badge of honor, refusing to let it go. This is a defiance of change and the burden this resistance brings into our lives weighs us down in all facets of life. It severely limits us creatively as well as getting in the way of enjoying healthy, loving relationships.

Like the passage of our childhood, that was once our reality but ultimately disappears, so too does our adult world change. The landscape of our life changes more quickly as we age, which demands that we adjust with resilience in a quicker and more effective way. This brings us back to the timeless wisdom of the willow.

The timely reminder the willow offers us is to remain in the present moment of our lives. Don't dwell in the shadows of the past with broken limbs of loss and regrets over what was, or could, or should have been. This will not sustain or bring us happiness in the present. Instead, let us apply the lessons of the willow when the winds subside. For it is here, in the winds of change, that the willow's branches straighten up, as the roots remain firmly anchored to the earth and the tree continues its upward growth to meet the sky and sun above.

## ROCKHAVEN MOMENTS

Moving my mother into Rockhaven established boundaries between her and me that were never there before. We may have had our issues over the years, but we were always involved with one another in some way. The advancing dementia and her new life at Rockhaven created clear and distinct lines between my mother's life and my own. New scenarios and interactions between us foreshadowed a future where I would be in this world without my mother. She was still physically alive, but there was less and less self-awareness for her, which meant our conversations were nothing like we used to have. For example, when I would come to visit her, which was often, she would routinely say she was ready to go home. She thought we were on a holiday at a nice hotel.

After wrangling with the guilt of having to lie to my mother, I learned how to handle this by replying to her, "Ma, we paid for the night so we might as well have dinner and go home tomorrow." This made sense to her and she would cease to ask about it, that is, until the next time I came to visit.

There were many visits that after asking me "How are you?" she would pick up on my hesitancy to answer her right away. In those lucid moments she was quick to point out, "It's taking you too long to answer. What's wrong?" With a false sense of hope and joy I would say to myself, "Yes, here is my mother, she knows me." I

*One moment, my darling Mother Charming of my adult years was there, coherent in all her illuminating brilliance, only to be replaced by the overbearing mother of my younger years and then, without warning, both versions were gone.*

would rush to tell her my problem believing for those brief seconds I was actually going to receive her advice. One sentence into my explanation of what was going on in my life and she would lose track of the conversation.

Sometimes, she would look away and say nothing. Other times she would angrily snap at me and ask, "What are you talking about? I don't understand a word you are saying. You aren't making any sense. What's wrong with you?" It was very difficult to remain in the present moment when this happened as her demeanor was reminiscent of the conversations we had during my growing up years, where in her eyes, I was regularly wrong or selfish. These trips to the past were becoming less and less frequent for me as they were replaced with what I referred to as the "Rockhaven Moments". They felt like I had just crashed into a solid wall at 100 miles an hour. One moment, my darling Mother Charming of my adult years was there, coherent in all her illuminating brilliance, only to be replaced by the overbearing mother of my younger years and then, without warning, both versions were gone.

For my mother these interactions would not be remembered the next day; let alone the next hour or preceding moments of them occurring. But, I never forgot them and it broke my heart. Especially the lies I needed to tell her regarding my father. She would ask me "Where's Daddy?" At first I would say, "Remember, Ma, Daddy's dead?" She would shutter and be alarmed as if this were new information to her. The loss of her beloved husband and the mourning of his passing would start afresh. It didn't take many of these instances for me to stop answering her honestly. There was no more pretending on my part about what she could handle. Nothing was going to pull her back into the now or any semblance of normal. Our relationship and our lives were forever changed.

During this time, I often found myself back to that moment as a five year old wondering who will love me and want me after my mommy leaves. Daddy was dead. Freddy the Frog was long gone and my recent divorce left me with a blank canvass upon which to paint my life's masterpiece. The question was, "what kind of life was I going to paint for myself?" I had no idea of the details or how this new beginning would take shape for me or my mother. Holding fast and true to my mother's wisdom that all would work out, I kept reminding myself that I was born under a lucky star, a thought my mother had instilled in me when I was young.

Here I was recently divorced, with a burgeoning acting career, and my biggest cheerleader, my best friend and confidant, was sliding deeper and deeper into a void from which she would never return. To reinterpret this situation and let go of what I could not change reminded me of the tenacity of a mouse in the maze, who never gets discouraged when there's no cheese down that hole. As it relentlessly pursues what it knows is going to satisfy its hunger, the mouse does not waste time where there is no food. For me, I was already well on my way to satisfying a life-long hunger to be a working actor. But who would cheer me on now? Who could I confide in? Who would be there to offer an inspirational reminder when it mattered most? My Mother Charming was gone. As emotionally troubling as this was, I could not stand idly by and lament what was an uncontrollable situation. I had to keep moving.

## *GRATITUDE MAKES CHANGE EASIER*

My father was the cheering section for me and my mother when he was alive. He was the one who would lovingly dote on me and my mother. It took me many years to understand why my mother stopped painting after my father passed away. It wasn't until the process of writing this book that I realized she stopped painting because she had lost her biggest fan.

As I look back on this period of my life, I realize now that so much of the trouble I had with my mother's declining health stemmed from fully accepting I was losing my biggest fan. Sure, we had challenging moments in our lives but in the most recent years before her health deteriorated we had enjoyed a renaissance in our relationship. She genuinely supported and acknowledged me on a level I'd always dreamed of. I had finally reclaimed "My Blue Heaven" but now it was slipping away again. I couldn't lie to myself about the realities of this situation. It was time to be present and accept the changes in our lives that I could not change, even if I desperately wanted to.

*Acceptance of change often comes slowly and always arrives hand in hand with self-preservation.*

Change is not easy. You come into the world alone and you go out the same way. No one can help you accept change, experience grief, or move on from loss. You must do these for yourself. The debilitating change in my mother's health and overall quality of life showed me that I needed to stop putting energy into resisting situations I didn't want and choose to put my creative energy into what it is I do want. This required me to first place a focus on being grateful for the beautiful experiences we shared rather than try and turn back the clock, thinking that her health would improve and we'd relive those moments again.

Acceptance of change often comes slowly and always arrives hand in hand with self-preservation. And self-preservation is a reliance on an outdated belief in the myth of scarcity. To no longer be attached to this myth means we must gratefully let go of what we once thought was our safety net. Our lives are enriched when we use gratitude to create space to entertain fresh, new ideas, which lead us to new people and new experiences. Being grateful for all my mother and I had gone through played a huge role in moving through what was an impossible to imagine series of life-altering scenarios. For as long as I could remember she was my safety net. Faced with a unique moment to create a new and infinitely more fulfilling life, I began to transition from a mode of surviving to a state of thriving.

So here was my fragile mother, a shell of her former self. There is nothing more I can say or do to change my mother's condition or situation, as much as I wished there were. When it was hopeless beyond my influence or power to fix or change or affect, it was necessary for me to gratefully let go. With my head held high and my life safe within my own hands, I surrendered control of an outcome that was never mine to begin with.

# Chapter 8

# ~ MY MOTHER, MY BEST FRIEND ~

*"God Bless the Child That Has Its Own."*
*Billie Holiday*

The doctors are pressing me for an immediate response on whether my mother lives or dies. My answer requires me to fill out a set of forms and check the appropriate boxes. Each second that is passing feels like an eternity. Is it really possible that our entire lives, regardless of what we accomplish, is ultimately decided by a check mark in a small box?

Here I was in a truly life or death moment. The whole core of my body felt heavy and numb. Blackness filled up all the spaces where I had held my hope that this hospital stay would work out for the best. My usually confident and unshakable self was gone. No carefully rehearsed smile could cloak my anguish.

I first learned how to act by watching my mother play different roles over the years for public show. It wasn't that she was hiding something or being disingenuous. The parents of our generation were required by society to act as if things were always going good, even in those moments when they weren't. She never confided in others. In her unique way my mother instilled in me early on that life is but a stage and to survive the role you were given, you better practice keeping your personal thoughts to yourself. When the curtains go up and you're in front of an audience, learn how to put on one helluva performance.

So, here I am on the grand stage of life, having to make the biggest decision I've ever faced. I take a deep breath, accepting the responsibility as her daughter, as her power of attorney. I open my mouth to tell the doctors what to do. But no words come out. I am not ready to make that decision. I must go back into my mother's room and see her.

*IN LIMBO*

Standing there, in the hallway of the hospital, waiting for the elevator doors to open, on this emotionally gut wrenching day, I honestly have to say I didn't think through what my life would be like without a family. The idea that this is an all too familiar situation for Baby Boomers never crossed my mind. For me, I was alone in all of this and no one could ever imagine what I was going through. I never really gave any thought to how tough it is to be truly alone because my mother and I were always in each other's lives.

What I had just placed on hold with the doctors could not wait any longer. Like it or not, I was front and center for my mother's inevitable passing and I wasn't at all sure I could handle this. With virtually no one to turn to for advice, the more rational and logical side of my personality kicked in at this moment. Maybe I should seek additional counsel from a plethora of doctors? Or maybe do something I'd never done much of to that point, which is go further inward and take in the word of God?

I found myself returning to what the doctor had said earlier in the day. Any further procedures would not do any good for a woman who had an advanced case of dementia, kidney failure and high blood pressure as my mother had. So here I am, the only child, with power of attorney, the only one left to make a decision to either prolong her life or end it sooner than later. The only thing I was sure of at this point was I was not going to put an old woman in her drastic condition on dialysis and stick a feeding tube into her stomach just to keep her alive.

For so much of my life I'd been raised on rules and belief systems, rooted in the misunderstanding of the past, as a means to prepare for a future that never seemed to arrive as it was envisioned. I can hear the words, "Make the butterfly fly," getting louder and the arrival of the moment when those words would have to be accepted without exception for my mother's life.

Despite what I thought I knew for sure, I remained in limbo between the unsure realities of two worlds. One rooted in the past, and in the impossible to know reality, projected into the future. I was leapfrogging the one reality that mattered – the present. This was the one that required a decision. And I just couldn't give one, not yet anyway.

## I CAN'T DO THAT

Riding up the elevator, I am drawn back to my memories of being a little girl and how I placed my mother on such a high pedestal. It seemed there was nothing she couldn't do, while I was convinced there was very little I could ever do that measured up to her. What was an impossible task for me was completed in the blink of an eye by my mother. I would excitedly clap my little hands and exclaim in wonder, "Wow,

Mommy, you can do that?" Shaking my head I would always add, "I can't do that."

My mother would smile at me, and in those moments I could feel her love. In my mind, the very act of her doing something for me that was outside my capabilities was an act of love. Like so many of my beliefs and interactions with my mother, this carried over to every area of my life as I grew older. For the better part of my life, if someone did what I needed to have done, even if I could perfectly do it for myself, the hidden message I interpreted was, "I am loved because someone did this for me". This came to have a reverse effect later in my life, from which I would learn a valuable lesson. The idea of letting someone else do something for me sounds good until I was faced with the realization that my self-worth is tied up in what others can do, as opposed to believing enough in my own gifts and skills. There is a healthy balance to strike between receiving the help of others and being in control of my own destiny. Never was this more apparent than in that moment riding in the hospital elevator.

So here I am, being pressured by doctors and my own internal knowingness of the severity of my mother's situation, to make a decision for my mother that involves both of our destinies. Couldn't she overcome this, I wondered? Where was my "super hero" mother when I needed her? Oh, right, she's the one in the hospital room incapacitated and incapable of doing anything for herself. With no one to depend on but myself, I couldn't help but wonder if I was prepared to make such a decision.

I'd managed to get through the change that occurred when mother was taken to the nursing home and now I am searching for ways to find the same resolve to get through this situation as I did then. I just couldn't shake the finality of this moment. As I face the unmistakable reality that it is always better to be *Despite my conflicting emotions and the time sensitive nature of making a decision, I find myself looking into the rearview mirror of our past.* able to do for yourself and not be dependent on others to do for you, I am reminded of the song lyrics from Billie Holiday's, *God Bless The Child*, which are, "Mama may have, Papa may have, But God bless the child that's got his own."

I'd accepted my mother's physical condition and I was thankful I could interact with her in brief moments of her

132

lucidity. But in this moment of change, this moment of choice, there was no more going back and forth between hope and despair. This was it. I am asked to end a life that I could not help but be infinitely grateful for, and so very much didn't want to let go of.

In these internally tense moments, before I have to make my decision final, I find myself engaged in a brief walk down memory lane. So many good times, so many sad ones too. A mixed bag really. I came up with a last ditch effort to untangle myself from the obvious emotional overwhelm that comes at a moment like this. Despite my conflicting emotions and the time sensitive nature of making a decision, I find myself looking into the rearview mirror of our past.

Where to start with the memories? Oh, yes, the little girl. There I am, so pretty, innocently hopeful and completely unaware of the compromises and sacrifices that lurked around the corner of my life. How is it that the incapable little girl, who at one point couldn't seem to do anything without her mother's help, is now the one who has to make a decision about whether she lives or dies? In these final moments before I would enter my mother's hospital room, all I kept hearing in my head was this little girl's voice say, "I can't do that."

## THE INFERIORITY COMPLEX

The elevator doors open and I make my way in the direction of my mother's hospital room. Never had I wished more than now to have someone to lean on. Despite the ups and downs she and I endured over the years, my mother was and remains a source of wonder and inspiration to me. Growing up, I looked upon her in amazement, her resiliency and creativity was a constant reminder of what she could do that I could not.

Placing my mother on such a high pedestal, feeling I was never able to fully satisfy her lofty standards, meant I saw myself as inferior. On the inside, I struggled with the concept of seeing my inner Prince Charming, for I had worked tirelessly throughout my adolescence and adulthood seeking her approval, even when she may have had no idea what I was doing. Truth is, I had no idea what I was doing, as I was seeking for something outside of myself that was always within me.

In my mind I was always trying to measure up to my mother. This prevented me from living in the present moment. It also erected a barrier between who I am and who I thought I had to be in order to be accepted. I am not

134

ashamed to say that I missed out on truly enjoying many of my life's accomplishments. That is not the case today, but it sure was during a good portion of my life.

The inferiority complex was a huge driving force in my life. Even now, as I write this book, it is not far from my mind and heart that I want to do right by my mother. It is not easy  sharing some of the painful moments of our time together as openly as I am, just as it was not easy that day walking out of the elevator and knowing what decision awaited me.

## IS THERE SOMETHING WRONG WITH YOU?

Rounding the corner in the hallway of the hospital, I see her room up ahead. Memories from our past wash over me like an emotional tsunami wave. As I approached the room, I vividly remember hearing my mother call out to me. Except it's not at the hospital, it is long ago.

I am in first grade and I'd just come home from school. No sooner do I put my school items on the table then my mother is beckoning me to her art room. Mother is a brilliantly gifted artist, more so than even she would have admitted. This was long before the passing of my father, which is when she inexplicably stopped painting. During this time of my life, painting was her passion. The colors she paints shine, laid down with skill and confidence, not mudded by rework or indecision. She is a creative force of nature, a perfectionist. And she expected perfection from me.

I timidly stand in the doorway of her art room. From behind her painting easel my mother says, "I went to see your first grade teacher today. I expected Mrs. George to tell me what a little genius I had sent to school. Much to my surprise, Mrs. George tells me that you are not ready to read yet. When I was in the first grade, Joan, I could read everything."

Remembering this experience opens a gateway to a rapid succession of memories, which flood my awareness as I move down the hallway of the hospital. It's now second grade and I am at Parent Night with my mother and father. My friend Phyllis comes up to me. She is always so jovial and wants me to hang out with her. I am very intent upon showing my parents my desk, so I brush past her.

My mother trains her intimidating gaze on me, "That little girl came up to you with love in her heart and you pushed her away. Look what you did to her, Joan." My mother's words and the disappointment on her face shot an arrow into my soul. I didn't think I had done anything wrong, but I must have, because my mother said so. Upsetting my mother was equivalent to dying for me. The next day, I didn't look at Phyllis or play with her.

I spent a good portion of my time as a child playing at home alone. On occasion, I would play with Georgie and his older sister, Joann, the kids next door. But other than those two, the children I would interact with were few and far between. I recall one evening sitting at the dining room table when my mother picked up her fork saying, "Your father and I don't understand why you don't have any friends. When we were your age, we always had a best friend and you don't." Without speaking another word, or an indication she expected me to answer, she began eating her dinner.

I looked down at my dinner plate but put no food in my mouth. Instead I was filled with shame and overwhelmed with a concrete belief that there is something wrong with me. Other children didn't want to play with me. I didn't know how to be a friend. These poisonous beliefs impacted me and my interaction with others for most of my life. It would take many years to fully unravel and reconcile the emotional impact this had on me.

*HOW DO I LOOK?*

These intense, life or death moments involving our parents bring our past front and center in ways we don't desire or plan. Nonetheless, we are required to make room for new experiences by gratefully letting go of the old ones we had bottled up. Making room for a new life allows us to clearly see just how much excess baggage we have been carrying around without being consciously aware of it.

> *"Joan, you are good looking enough for all normal purposes."*

Nowhere was this more apparent to me and more relevant for my life and my mother's than it was on that day in the hospital. It was the amalgamation of all the experiences she and I have had. Here they were rising to the surface of my mind and engulfing my heart, literally forcing me to confront the realities of a relationship I'd long felt, but did not quite fully understand. Needing to come to a clear consensus in my mind as to what to do with my mother's life, I found myself wondering how different and hurdle-free my life's development could have been, if only she had been more nurturing and complimentary when I needed her support.

I recall a seminal moment during my senior year in high-school. I whirl around in front of my mother in my party dress, "How do I look?" My mother looks me up and down and says a line from the play, Our Town, "Joan, you are good looking enough for all normal purposes." Do I listen to my internal instincts and buy into the negativity? Or do I bask in the ambiance of her smile and attention, no matter how fleeting it is? Truth is, her words punctured a hole through my heart in a way I could never let my mother know. I didn't realize how much this affected me because I had already trained myself to not feel or show the inflicted wounds, but just keep moving through life.

I deftly shift to another question in hopes of getting a favorable response, "Ma, how do you like the dress I am wearing tonight to the party?"

"Joan, you haven't finished sewing it. You can't wear it like that."

"Ma, I know it's not exactly done. I basted it and have safety pins holding it together. But I really want to wear it to the party tonight and it will be fine," I explain.

"Joan, you never finish anything," she says as her eyes are no longer on me but back to the magazine she was reading before I entered the room.

"Yes I do," knowing this is true, but internally doubting my own conviction.

Without lifting her eyes from the magazine she states, "No you don't, Joan. And I hope the dress falls apart on you tonight." The dress did not fall apart and I had a wonderful time at the party. Despite this, the interaction between us was never far from my mind that night or all of the days and nights that would follow.

*AN UNHEALTHY COMPETITION*

That day at the hospital I was overcome with something I had felt the intensity of but rarely stopped to consider: the competition between my mother and myself. Years later, as I immersed myself further into the *Drive-Thru, Make It Your Own®* campaign and this book, it became clear to me that one of the things very few people openly speak of is the unhealthy nature of this competition between parents and their children. Nowhere was this more overtly felt and displayed than for Boomers.

Baby Boomers on a whole are quite fortunate to have had parents who genuinely wanted the best for their children. That wasn't always the case with several of the generations that came before us. It's not to sugarcoat our generation's upbringing either; because in no way, shape or form did we have it easy. I am living proof that the expectations and ideas of success passed on by our parents, particularly the mothers of the Baby Boomer daughters, was harshly predicated on their rigid dictates and a micro-management oversight of our lives.

One could argue, our parents did the best they could with what they knew. I agree. But did we learn enough from our parent's mistakes, and our own, to not pass them on to the next generation to needlessly repeat what we had to endure? Boomers have clearly learned a lot from our past errors and successes. The question is, how can we impart this wisdom to younger generations if we keep clinging to the notion that everything was so wonderful during a time when our parents struggled with their own lives on a level few care to admit?

Could we, as a generation, have truly changed the world in the ways we really wanted to if we had not been in competition with our parents? How different would our world have been if our parents had not placed us on the

141

receiving end of covert daggers and arrows, disguised as helpful advice, each one targeting a soft, vulnerable developing side of our fragile little personalities? What could we have accomplished if we had been nurtured in a way that reinforced how important and beautiful we are? Writing this now, I am reminded of Abileen, the loving black nanny in the book and movie "The Help", who fondly tells the little white girl she cares for, Mae Mobley, "You is kind. You is smart. You is important."

On that life-altering day for me in the hospital, these memories of growing up and so many more lessons from my past, replayed in my head. They were appearing to me in what I felt was an inopportune moment. But looking back, knowing that it was all exquisitely timed, I needed to face the ghosts of my past, forgive the hidden grievances, let go of the lost sense of innocence and forgive myself and my mother for the hurt and confusion of a competitive relationship that was a symbol of my own inner competition with myself.

My mother was everything to me. To bring all of what we had experienced together into a singular moment of self-acceptance, in a way that allowed me to transmute these long repressed feelings and embrace what had transpired over so many years, gave me the confidence to finally step into the beautiful woman my mother always wanted for me, but didn't know how to show it.

Perhaps, all of what we'd experienced together was designed to bring me to this moment so that I could fully appreciate who I am and be more grateful for my mother than I already was. By seeing past the flaws I imagined to be within me, I was able to begin recognizing the perfection of my own imperfection. Could it be that I was more prepared for making this life-changing decision for my mother and myself than I had given myself credit for?

## FILLING THE VOID

The nurturing side of my mother was counterbalanced with a short, abrupt nature that created numerous tense moments. As harsh as my mother could be at times, she was an incredibly giving and compassionate soul. She had an innate understanding of how to prepare me for situations in my life that could be perceived as troubling for a young child. While I was young, she would always be sure to read to me or come up with wonderfully imaginative stories, creatively weaving in something relevant that I would soon be facing in my life.

This never ceased to calm me and infuse an added strength and confidence I had not previously felt.

Whatever challenges we faced, my mother always made sure to have my back when others felt I was less than deserving of anything. One incident I couldn't help but laugh at was how she never forgot what my high school counselor, Mr. Bregoli, once said to my mother and me.

*To this day, "You're born under a lucky star," remains the single most important thing she ever said to me.*

We were in his office reviewing colleges and asked for his input as to which one he felt would be best suited for me. His response was that I was not "college material." That infuriated my mother. Upon graduating from the University of California, Berkeley my mother writes an article about my graduation that was published in the local newspaper. She personally delivers a copy to Mr. Bregoli, along with a few choice words.

Whether it was Mr. Bregoli, friends at school, interactions with customers at my own business or specifically, my mother, I never allowed anyone to see where these arrows had deflated my self-confidence. I did an excellent job of masking my internal torture well enough that people didn't see anything but a highly confident woman. I overcompensated for my lack of self-worth with a fierce competitiveness and unshakable determination that I could get whatever I wanted if I set my mind to it. I was, after all, born under a lucky star, as my mother very early on instilled in me.

I stop mid-way down the hallway, my eyes fixed on the door to my mother's hospital room. All these thoughts that had been racing through my mind dissipate but the one that matters. She is more than just my mother. She was and will forever remain my best friend. To this day, "You're born under a lucky star," remains the single most important thing she ever said to me. For when all was said and done, the way in which my mother loved me and how she came to prepare me for my life, I have nothing but the utmost love and gratitude for this gift.

# Chapter 9

# ~ CHASING YOUTHFUL SHADOWS ~

*"Youth is happy because it has the capacity to see beauty.*
*Anyone who keeps the ability to see beauty never grows*
*old."*
*Franz Kafka*

When were we ever young? It seems the older we get in age the more we contemplate and even lament the lost days of our youth. Let us consider that in our journey through the memories of our youth we are overlooking the value of our most important moment of life, which is the present. While we may not have considered the present moment and age we are right now as being the youngest we will ever be, it actually is. Can we accept this reality or must we continue to search for a time that has long since passed us by?

If we do go in search of that elusive image of our youth who is to say that somewhere in the not so distant future we will be looking back on our lives wondering how we could have overlooked how good we had it right now. And isn't the lesson of our past not to repeat the mistakes we so carelessly made in our youth? If we are the youngest right now we will ever be consider how important it is to our quality of life to enjoy the time we have right now, rather than waste it worrying about a future that hasn't arrived and searching for a past that will never come back.

As time unfolds, many of us fall into a trap of trying in vain to reach back into a timeless void to reclaim a semblance of our youth. What we are seeking is an experience that is intricately bound in the physical. What this means is that our search to remain forever young is underscored by the belief that the younger our bodies are the younger our state of mind is. However, Pablo Picasso was fond of saying that, "youth is ageless". Is this true or have we fooled ourselves about age and youth based on what we've been led to believe by the media, advertisement and the entertainment industries?

## THE VOID BETWEEN PAST AND PRESENT

A variety of studies conducted on the correlation between one's thoughts and our physical health have revealed how we think of ourselves has a significant impact on our ability to prolong a youthful and active life. But, this has nothing to do with wishful nostalgia. For example, there is a well-known study overseen by National Cancer Institute research psychologist, Sandra Levy, Ph.D., which revealed women who expressed more joy in their lives tend to live a longer, healthier life. This was part of a seven-year follow-up of breast cancer patients that helped further reinforce the direct role our mind has on the body.

Although these studies can help sharpen our frame of reference for important areas of our lives, none of them are going to show how, or even why, we can gratefully fill this apparent void between the past and present. The answer for that is accepting  no matter how much we wish for the youthful past to resurrect itself, we are not going to miraculously replace our current physical body with the one of our youth. What these studies illustrate, then, is the more we stay in the joyous experiences of our present lives the higher quality of life we're going to have right now. This does not mean we should refrain from enjoying the feeling of fond memories from our youth. There is a lot of fun to be had when we look back at experiences of our younger self. Where we get into trouble is when we get caught up in the fruitless battle to reclaim a part of ourselves that is long gone.

Without being aware of what we are doing to ourselves we are easy prey to fall into the manipulative trap the media, advertisement and entertainment industries set up for us when it comes to our youth. If we are convinced the past was better than the actual reality of what we experienced, and we buy into the stories that our future is a giant pitfall of potential calamities, we will extinguish our resources, financially, emotionally, spiritually and physically, in order to transport ourselves back in time. Of course, we don't actually travel back in time, but in a very real sense

> *We owe it to ourselves to get on with our youthful self and enjoy where we are at this stage of our lives.*

we do so in our mind, and this exacerbates the blind spot that causes us to overlook the fulfillment of our dreams in the present moment.

In his book, *The Zahir,* author Paulo Coelho suggests that we are prisoners of personal history. He says, "Everyone believes that the main aim in life is to follow a plan. They never ask if that plan is theirs or if it was created by another person. They accumulate experiences, memories, things, other people's ideas, and it is more than they can possibly cope with. And that is why they forget their dreams."

To be fair, none of us are immune from chasing the youthful shadows of our past. We may have been younger looking, faster and stronger than we are today, but do our physical attributes define us? We owe it to ourselves to get past our youthful self and enjoy where we are at this stage of our lives. But in order to do this it will be necessary to accept who we are and no longer define ourselves with the false stories presented to us through outside influences such as the media, advertisement and entertainment industries.

## GLAMORIZING THE PAST

To better understand how we are programmed to search for something or someone to fill the void within us, it is necessary we not overlook both the intent and enormity of the investment in resources called upon by the media, advertising and the entertainment industries to glamorize the past and paint a gloom and doom picture of the future for Boomers. Hundreds of billions of dollars in revenue and tens of thousands of jobs are generated through Boomers being distracted from the lives we have today, and we're not the only ones whose focus is redirected from our present day reality.

The way this distraction takes place is how the stories, products and services aimed at consumers are overtly framed around our physical capabilities and looks, making it seem all but impossible to see ourselves as youthful. Getting caught up in these nostalgic tales of what we no longer have can be emotionally and mentally unhealthy. This is particularly true when we allow ourselves to equate our joy with a physical set of attributes that are impossible to return to in our later years. Without stripping away this illusion we will continue to buy into the myth of aging, convinced our youth was better than it really was.

A few fun experiences here and there do not make our past better than where we are now. The reality of this, however, does not stop many Boomers from conveniently recalling one or two incidents in their youth and using them as the primary basis for why their life is not as good today.

While it can be quite fun delving into nostalgic fantasies, it is important for us to be aware that the further we get away from appreciating our lives in the present, the less clear some of the experiences of our past end up being. The reason for this is that the murky details of the past, some of which carry a lot of pain we do not want to remember, can make us susceptible to making up stories about our life that have

151

nothing to do with what we really experienced. The intent of pulling the wool over our own eyes is directly attributed to our refusal to both accept and take responsibility for our present day realities.

In our younger days we were so caught up trying to break free from the strict constraints of society's rules and prove ourselves worthy of love, that the struggles we went through to succeed on our terms are one giant blur. In fact, many of those struggles carry so much trauma that it is easier to make up a better life than the one we went through. It is here we end up passing on the myths we were raised with and battled against, to future generations. This happens because we buy into the need of thinking that the struggles we went through were all worth it because we had fun with the process. In our youth we were not focused on the present, as our eyes were on the so-called "prize". This guarantees we were not enjoying the process and thus, we forget what we were struggling against and lose sight on what we were really attempting to achieve.

When the media, advertisement and entertainment industries paint an entirely different picture of where we came from with a glossy façade, set to the musical soundtrack of our youth, it is easy to idolize our past. Placing our youth on some idealistic pedestal overshadows the lessons of our earlier days. Rather than passing on our lessons to future generations, in order not to repeat them, we reinforce the very myths that were at the heart of our struggles. And when the younger generation sees the need to change the course of their lives, because they do not want to follow in our footsteps, it causes many Boomers to look at the younger generations of today with disdain, believing they are not grateful for what they have. But it is our generation that seems ungrateful with where we are and how good we actually have it. For if we were grateful there would be little to no need to hide from our past by creating a version of it that never really existed to begin with.

Creating a division between generations and prompting us to look at our past with envy, this is the true intent of the stories and advertising campaigns we are bombarded with. When we are distracted by outside pursuits, we fail to see the power we have within us and we unknowingly give away our power and sense of self-worth to services and products that can't possibly satisfy our craving to feel loved and acknowledged. There is nothing wrong with buying products and services to improve our lives. Therefore, if we are to truly live our best life, we should be willing to admit that nothing will satisfy us until we accept we are worthy of the inner Prince Charming we so valiantly seek validation from with outside pursuits.

*THE NOSTALGIA GENERATION*

Despite a focus on seeking to reclaim past glories, the pleasures of our current age can be directly attributed to being smarter now. One unmistakable trait about our generation is that we know how to have fun without confusing activity with accomplishment. Many of us are more financially solvent than most of society and thankfully, we have the experience and wisdom to tell the truth from a lie. But, is any of this actually true?

Considering the bleak financial and health issues many Boomers have unexpectedly encountered, many would say we cannot afford to celebrate our lives right now. Still, there is no denying that our wisdom of today far exceeds what we used to think we knew, in the bliss of our youthful ignorance. But what good is this wisdom if it is tossed aside in favor of believing false stories we are told by outside forces, whose sole intent is to profit off our unwillingness to let go of something no longer there?

I'm not suggesting that all Baby Boomers are focused on the past or frightened of the future. Nor am I saying that we should overlook and deny our financial responsibilities and health. But, it would be foolish for any of us to think there is not a large percentage of the Baby Boomer population hypnotized by nostalgic myths that are doing more harm than good.

If we're going to spend so much of our time and resources on nostalgia, it behooves us to be clear on what our past really looked like. This is a dangerous game of denial we are playing, when we allow ourselves to be hypnotized by an illusion of our past that didn't really exist the way we're told it did. And, it's not just Baby Boomers being sold on the myths of the past, or that being physically young is where life is truly enjoyed. The whole world is being sold on these lies. It's inconceivable then, to think only Boomers are negatively affected by what the media, advertising and entertainment industries are doing to profit off the myths of scarcity and reinforcing the belief that aging is a disease we must avoid at all costs.

When we can let go of our need to be mesmerized by our past, and reconcile all of the contradictory beliefs that support it, it is very easy to see what drives the industries whose source of profit is selling the seven myths to society. In breaking these myths we cannot deny that we Boomers

our need to keep holding onto myths that we know are not in our best interest?

Only when these companies realize that they can profit from our wisdom, will their campaigns and stories change. Therefore, it is not enough to try and change the outside world from what we think is not working. We must first look within and change what we feel we are worthy of experiencing. And only when we realize it is okay for us to enjoy our lives without feeling guilty or ashamed for bucking the status quo, will our story change. That is precisely where Boomers, as the largest segment of the world's population, can exercise our strength in numbers by changing not only our belief in scarcity but how aging can be celebrated, rather than shrouded in disease and fear. But, until our generation can look beyond our past and let go of the grief, anger and guilt from the immense losses we have had to endure, our wisdom is not a gift but a curse.

> *Only when we realize it is okay for us to enjoy our lives without feeling guilty or ashamed for bucking the status quo, will our story change.*

The era we grew up in, both as children and adults, forced us to deal with some agonizing losses. We've lost family members, friends, spouses and children. Add in the enormous financial losses and health crisis many are dealing with right now and it seems impossible to escape the myth of scarcity. What makes all of this harder to deal with is that much of our present day struggles are the result of how we lived in our youthful, carefree days. Our generation built up an incalculable mountain of debt, the least of which was financial.

## COULD'VE, SHOULD'VE, WOULD'VE

As we get closer to the end of our lives it is not uncommon to run through the inventory of our life experience and end up overwhelmed with a bunch of thoughts that start with, "I could've, should've and would've." This is precisely what the media, advertising and entertainment industries feed off of. We are regularly told the mistakes of our past will be repeated if we do not buy specific services or products. Simultaneously, we are told we do not live in a world of abundance and yet there is more abundance available to all of us than ever before. This is where the gift of our wisdom is needed the most.

We never believed we were going to age, so the long-term consequences of the creative risks we took when we were younger were never factored in. This brings us back to the idea of loss. It's not just our dear loved ones we have lost along the way. We lost a lot of our athleticism and many activities we used to be proficient in during our younger days have diminished. The physical limits we are facing today may seem to paint a helpless picture of our present circumstances.

*We have the wisdom to forgive ourselves for what we think we did wrong and this applies to letting go of grievances for those we believe have wronged us.*

For instance, if we need to secure a new and better paying job, physical limitations and our age will be nearly impossible to overcome. In the area of dating and romance, this too can seem to be quite a deterrent. But, if there is one thing we did not lose, as we got older, it is our wisdom, which we have an abundance of.

The value of wisdom is knowing we don't have all the time we once thought we had to undo whatever errors our youth racked up on the tab of life. This is why so few of us want to look into the future, because we fear the debt we have to pay for the things we messed up on. We look into the future and at our age we see more loss, which is something none of us want to experience. Instead, we look to the past where it seems we can create a new set of memories and escape the perceived horrors of what we believe is waiting for us around the corner.

Whether it's looking to the future or the past, if we undersell ourselves on the power and value of our wisdom, we're giving away the control we have to impact the most important moments of our lives. We have the wisdom to forgive ourselves for what we think we did wrong and this applies to letting go of grievances for those we believe have wronged us. Our wisdom, then, is used to remove the illusion of debt that we believe must be paid in the future for what went wrong in the past. And what is debt but a means to use the past as a justification to punish ourselves and others in the future? So, when we use our wisdom to remove debt we free ourselves up to enjoy our lives in the present, which is where the true value of living is.

When we love ourselves enough not to chase a better life in the past or look for it in other people and material items, there ceases to be any need for accumulating or paying of debt. Where there is no debt, there is no pressure to do things that are not in our best interest. We have in essence freed ourselves from feeling we owe anyone anything. Because we are not expecting anyone or anything else to fulfill us, there is no burdensome expectation to hold over anyone, especially ourselves. Herein lies the gift of our youth and the application of our wisdom.

# Chapter 10

## ~ NOW WHAT? ~

*"Listen to your intuition. It is the voice of your inner child and it is here to teach you."*

*Joanie Marx*

I am proposed to and my answer is, "Yes." My mother says, "Allan is the ugly duckling who will turn into a swan." My father sits in front of the television and says from behind his cigar smoke cloud, "Allan loves you, but I don't think you love him. And God help you when you do fall in love someday."

Not exactly the responses I was hoping for from my parents. Like all that I had learned up to that point in my life about survival, never show where the arrows pierced you. I say to myself, "But, Allan does love me and that is what's important."

We get married in a small ceremony and move to Ohio, where Allan returns to his graduate school studies. This is the furthest I've ever been from home. It is a new life and I should be adjusting well, but I am not. I sleep as much as 16 hours a day in some stretches.

162

Our apartment is small and while it is nicely furnished, not one piece of furniture has an armrest. We're living in a total armless furnished apartment. Often, I find this fact funny. But, it also reminds me that it is not just my parents or armrests I am without. I have no friends and no job. A new life I may have, but it is akin to having no life and this is devastatingly difficult to accept.

During my days when I am not sleeping, I ponder the prospect of returning to Berkeley to attend graduate school. On the day I intend to muster up enough courage to actually share my plans with Allan, the doorbell rings and there stands the UPS man with my 18 boxes filled with wedding gifts. The voice in my head says, "I can't leave now, my things have arrived. Now what?" The answer to this question became a journey into marriage and the creation of our future. Like it or not, it is time to settle into this new life and make the most of it.

## YOUR MOTHER ISN'T WORTH IT

You know how you can flip through a calendar and certain dates jump out at you because of their personal significance? For me November 8th never did, that is until the night I find myself under the blaze of emergency room lights in a hypertensive crisis. My blood pressure is 240/120. This is not a good number. Normal is 120/80 not 240/120, which is in the red zone at the top of the scale.

A little blood trickles out of my nose. Seeing your own blood, when it is unexpected, is scary. Under these intense circumstances it is downright frightening. I follow the directions of the nurse and put on the hospital gown. The nurse attaches electrodes to my chest for the continuous EKG. A blood pressure cuff is wrapped around my arm and automatically inflates every few minutes. I put a pill under my tongue to dilate my blood vessels. The nurse lays a blanket over me and calmly says, "Ma'am, we're admitting you to this hospital if your blood pressure doesn't come right down."

My heart pounds wildly and despite the nature of my condition, I resolve that I will not have a heart attack or a stroke. But, I am aware that the nurses think I might. One of the nurses comes up to me at this point and asks, "Would you like to call your husband?" She says this not so much as a question, but more so as an assumption. I didn't want to call Allan. I answer, "No, that won't be necessary. " The shock on the nurse's face is forever etched in my memory.

Two hours later, it is 1:00 am and my blood pressure is still dangerously elevated in the red zone. The nurse tries again, "Are you sure you don't want to call your husband?" This time it is said with a bit more urgency. "I can get you a phone. He must be worried sick about you." My answers become more of a battle within myself as to whether or not I divulge the real reason why I don't want to call. Maybe it would be best to simply act my way out of it. Having just come from acting class, I go with the latter.

*"I've been under a lot of stress lately. I thought I was handling it well, but I guess not."*

"Oh, no thank you, really no," I say, mustering up as much conviction as I can. "He knows I went to my Monday night acting class. I am sure he is sleeping and I don't want to wake him and worry him for no reason. But thank you for asking." The nurse buys the response, even if her expression indicates she doesn't agree with me.

I don't call my husband because it is drizzling outside, the streets are slick, he can't see well and I don't want him to risk driving to the hospital. Outside of being concerned for his safety, I don't want to hear his criticisms or feel his cold, aloof response, which would likely have been something along the lines of, "Look what you are doing to yourself. Your mother isn't worth it." It's not that I made up the response. It is what he has been repeatedly saying now for months. And I just couldn't bear to hear it one more time, especially on this night.

## THE WRITING IS ON THE WALL

I've been in the hospital now for over three hours. I am lying in the hospital bed pretending to be calm. Inside I am a nervous wreck. The on-call doctor enters the room, checks the monitors and looks me over, "What brought all of this on?" My answer does little to explain as I reply, "I've been under a lot of stress lately. I thought I was handling it well, but I guess not."

It's becoming clear to me as I lie there, that I haven't been handling things all that well in my life. My marriage is all but over, there are daily fires to put out at the business and the continuously rapid decline of my mother's health is tearing me apart. It's not really a matter of what stressful situations brought me into the hospital, but how I hadn't folded under the stress sooner. Perhaps the final straw had been the previous day, when I find out our biggest customer had just declared bankruptcy and we have lost a fortune because of it. I don't know what to do but state the obvious, even if it offers no help, "Well, Allan, this is the risk we take when we own our own business. We'll just have to make the money back someplace else."

Later that afternoon, all I could think about was getting to acting class, which has become my refuge where I can escape my downward spiraling reality for a few hours. On my way to class I caught myself saying, "Make the butterfly fly." The only time these words entered my mind was when I had exhausted all possibilities for creating a favorable outcome in a situation. At that moment, I was accepting that a huge part of my life was coming to an end. The only thing was I couldn't determine if it was in response to me seeing the end of our business, our marriage, my mother's health, or something else.

Fearfully, I look up at the monitors which are beeping. Finally, my blood pressure is coming down. I remind myself that I will not have a heart attack or stroke. And I refuse to become a mean, hateful, demented shell of a person, like my mother is now.

Discharged at 4:00 am, I promise the doctor and nurses I will see my family doctor first thing in the morning. I drive away with a handful of pills, none of which are capable of giving me the strength to pull my beloved mother back from her black abyss, refill our bank account with the money we lost the previous day or restore the illusion of my marriage.

I arrive home and tiptoe into the house. No sooner do I get into the kitchen and there stands Allan in his pajamas, barefoot, wearing an inquisitive and surprisingly concerned look on his face. He asks, "What happened to you?" We sit down at the dining room table. In a matter of fact way, I tell him what happened and where I'd been for the last several hours. We both know a solution is not going to be hashed out right then, but we are also wise enough to know the writing has been on the wall for a rather long time. The details will sort themselves out in the future. We go to bed. He lies on his side of the bed and I am on my mine. I sleep for the next six days.

*ME*

In between my waking moments during those six days, I can't escape the feeling of how this reminds me of the first few weeks we were in Ohio during the early stages of our marriage. Going back to college made sense at that time, but where would I go now? Is it even reasonable to assume I could survive on my own? One thought in particular brings a heavy dose of guilt: reconciling my choice in the hospital emergency room to accept the caring, uncritical attention of strangers over my own husband.

After the six days a strange thought occurred to me. There was something I had not fully articulated to myself before then, but nonetheless, I had felt its presence my whole life. It was the idea of Prince Charming. I found myself remembering those fairy tales my mother used to read to me from Golden Books. Oh, what I wouldn't give to return to those moments. Never had I needed my mother's soothing comfort as an adult more than I did right then, but she is literally a shell of her former, wondrous Mother Charming self.

I sit with the idea of Prince Charming and consider the impact those stories had on me and others who grew up with them. I know my experiences in life are unique to me, but I couldn't possibly be the only woman who bought into the fairytale of marrying Prince Charming. I find myself asking a familiar question, "Now what?" The answer didn't come with a package of explicit details of what to do or directions on where my life was headed, but it was clear enough. There is no turning back. I accept right then that I have to change my life.

I'm learning to fly and if I am to create "My Blue Heaven" on my terms it has to happen sooner rather than later. Little did I realize at the time, but along the way to creating "My Blue Heaven", I would meet a truly fascinating and beautiful person who is my Prince Charming. Me. Even so, in the years that follow the image and knowledge of me being my own Prince Charming often vanishes into black uncertainty. Truth be told, the idea of loving who I am is not easy.

*OUR STORY, OUR VOICE AND OUR TIME*

Although, I am more conscious of my choices today than ever before and I am aware that I am my own Prince Charming, the idea of accepting I am enough without outside validation is a difficult bridge to cross. Writing this book and the experience of being a Baby Boomer advocate has gone a long way to helping me shorten the distance between time spent seeking approval from others and accepting my own inner approval.

I am younger now than in any of my days to follow or in the moments I remember in my physical youth. It was not easy for me to embrace this truth, but I now refuse to spend my time wasting valuable energy holding people responsible for my happiness. My life today is the only moment I find value in rejoicing and celebrating. Like everyone else, I get with friends and reminisce about past experience. Even when I am alone, I smile at the recollection of memories I shared with my mother and others who came in and out of my youth. But, to yearn for such moments at the expense of my present life, does me a disservice. For what other moment am I going to be as young or find happiness in, than where I reside now?

*Youth is a state of mind, represented in the very being of who we are.*

Youth is a state of mind, represented in the very being of who we are. Far too long, we have allowed the media, advertising and entertainment companies to convince us that youth is locked away in a moment in time that we can never reclaim, except through products and services. When we allow others to determine what constitutes our youth or how beautiful and loved we are, we have given away far more than our money or wisdom. We have thrown away the very essence of who we truly are.

Today, we are smarter and more aware of life on a grander scale than any previous generation. Let us not overlook what we have learned about the pitfalls of living with a scarcity-based mindset by chasing after illusions of Prince Charming. It is up to us Baby Boomers to be an example to other generations that a quality life is not lived through scarcity, but through a mindset of abundance. We create the world we live in and it's time we take full ownership of our creative powers. This is our story. This is our voice. And this is our time.

# Chapter 11

## ~ DIVORCING THE PAST WITH GRATITUDE ~

*"Everything will be alright in the end. So if it's not alright,*
*it is not yet the end."*
*Deborah Moggach*

Like millions of Baby Boomers, I have tasted the bitterness of divorce. While many believe that divorce helps us erase our errors, in my experience, the one thing it doesn't erase is the past. And if we are not careful about the lessons of divorcing our past, we will be highly prone to repeating mistakes, in some cases at a much higher cost, both emotionally and financially.

In Neil Simon's play "Chapter Two" the lead character, Jennie, returns home from a trip to Jamaica after an attempt to erase the painful memories of her recent divorce. Her friend Faye joins her back in Jennie's apartment where she laments that place is filled with "the ghost of Gus's cigar…God, what a cheap thing to be haunted by." Jennie goes on to say, "I wasted five lousy years living with Gus trying to justify the one good year I had with him, all because

173

I wouldn't take responsibility for my own life. Dumb! You're dumb, Jennie Malone! All of us. We shouldn't get alimony, we should get the years back. Wouldn't it be great if just once the judge said, 'I award you six years, three months, two days and custody of your former youthful body and fresh glowing skin!'"

When any of us emerge from a divorce, the first thing we attempt to do is make up for what we believe is lost time. No matter our age, we want to turn back the clock and somehow regain a portion of our youth that has seemingly been wasted on a promise that never materialized. This is an attempt in futility. Trying to bring back a time that is long since gone ultimately backfires. This is because we invent all sorts of external distractions to find and correct something that is and will always be inside of us.

It is for this very reason that so many people find themselves moving from one divorce to the next, each time hoping that the new situation will prove to be better than the last. And, I am not just referring to the divorce of a marriage. The concept of divorce applies to removing dysfunctional thoughts and behavior out of our lives, which undoes the need to disguise our self-worth in other people, things or situations.

## REMOVING REGRET

In our haste to reinvent our youth into some nostalgic fantasy, we tend to dress up the mistakes of the past and forget the real purpose of being young. These mistakes are conveniently overlooked after a divorce, to the extent we don't even recognize we are repeating the same dysfunctional behavior at this stage of our lives that we did in our younger days. Except in this moment, we don't have the luxury of wasting time to correct these errors as we

> *Without being grateful for what we learned from our past, we end up repeating youthful mistakes we should have learned from by now.*

may have once been gifted. Like it or not, we are not getting any younger age wise, and the more years that we allow to pass by in denial, the more of our lives we are wasting.

We may feel younger after a divorce because we temporarily feel revived after having been freed from the shackles of a situation that did not seem to reach the promise it once held. The one thing we cannot escape is that the path we are on continues to present us with the same questions. Did I do the right thing? Am I really happier on this new path? And if *(fill in the blank)* happened, would it have worked out?

When we learn that the past is no longer our ally we can revitalize our lives in ways that leave our past completely unimaginable compared to how good we have it now. This is how it should be. But for so many Baby Boomers, this attempt at moving on doesn't reach the promise we believed it should, much like the marriage we just got a divorce from. So, where can we rejuvenate and revitalize our lives in a way that honors both the past, as much as it honors the beauty of our present moment? The answer is divorcing our past with gratitude.

Without being grateful for what we learned from our past, we end up repeating youthful mistakes we should have learned from by now. Our youthful past not only delivered us to the present, but it also taught us what didn't work and why. Regaining our youthful exuberance should not include making the same mistakes we did when we were younger and didn't know any better. Not knowing is an excuse we do not have the luxury of falling back on now. This is where the power of gratitude comes in.

If we are aware of what the past taught us, our gratitude for these lessons will vastly improve key areas of our lives and the burden of regret will be less prevalent. We will be able to look at our past through the lens of gratitude and no longer view mistakes of our youth as worthless. If our mistakes helped bring us to a better point in our lives, that means we learned from them. Therefore, gratitude removes regret for what we think was a waste of our youth, opening the door of possibility to create a higher quality of life for ourselves and others, when and where it matters. And nowhere does it matter more than now. It is here in the present moment where divorcing our past offers us peace of mind and frees us up to explore the depths of appreciation for who we are. For if we cannot appreciate our physical youth when we had it, how can we appreciate what it means to be the age we are in our present lives?

## THE FIFTH WHEEL

For a brief time after the divorce from Allan, I have heard the voices in my head saying the following: "She has a husband, she has a life, for she is the wife." This edict drummed into our heads from the past puts a wall of isolation around divorced or widowed older women. It intensifies the feeling of being the odd-person out, the fifth wheel. The intent is to shame us into obscurity for disrupting the status quo. This is not some unsubstantiated theory, for there are millions of women who have faced this in many different ways, including my mother.

I remember vividly my mother recalling an incident the year following my father's passing. It was her first trip on her own and she returned to The Laguna Hotel in Laguna Beach, California where she and my father had vacationed every year of

> *Stepping out of a marriage is as much about divorcing a lifestyle that does not fit who we are, as it is divorcing the person we're married to.*

their marriage. During her stay there was a devastating moment when she was reminded how society in general tends to treat women of her age when they are not accompanied by a man. She was exiting the hotel and a couple were walking directly in front of her. The couple reached the exit first and the man opened the door for his wife, but chose not to do so for my mother, letting it slam back in her face. My father not only would have grabbed the door and held it open for my mother, but it is quite likely my mother would not have been invisible, had my father or any other man been with her.

While my mother's experience can be seen as an isolated incident, it is not relegated to just women of a certain age. Stepping out of a marriage is as much about divorcing a lifestyle that does not fit who we are, as it is divorcing the person we're married to. Often times, this divorce of a lifestyle is not from one's own doing, as was the case for my mother and others who are widowed. No matter the cause behind the end of a marriage, the adjustment from one lifestyle to a new one leaves many people feeling like a fifth wheel when they are around other couples. But this is not the only place in which the fifth wheel is felt. It also happens when we leave careers or move out of a social situation we had been in for a long time.

Those who remain in situations and lifestyles where we once were tend to both consciously and unconsciously, exclude us from activities. To change this will require an overhaul of how we were raised to see ourselves, as much as it is reinterpreting what it means to genuinely offer compassion and gratitude to those whose life circumstances are suddenly different from our own. And this means undoing the past.

## THE PAST IS IMMUTABLE

Undoing the past is to break the myth that the status quo cannot be changed. In the world in which we were raised, society taught us to honor certain institutions of life, many of which were afforded a sacred status that was more important in sustaining, than the happiness of the people living within the confined walls of these institution's rules and myths. Marriage is one such sacred institution we were raised to never let go of.

During our parent's generation, and our own, to challenge the validity of a marriage or any of the other sacred institutions that made up society brought about shame and blame for attempting to change the status quo. This means men and women of our era had to assume very specific roles or risk being outcasts, not only in social circles, but our own families. For some these pre-determined roles fit them, but for many of us the roles of the past were not at all conducive to who we were then or relevant to who we became later in life. Poet and philosopher Omar Khayyam, who lived from 1048 to 1131, is well known for writing about the difficulties of undoing our past. In one of his more famous quotes he says:

*"The Moving Finger writes; and, having writ,*
*Moves on: nor all thy Piety nor Wit,*
*Shall lure it back to cancel half a Line,*
*Nor all thy Tears wash out a Word of it."*

On one end, the past is immutable and we cannot change anything we have experienced. But we must not overlook the thoughts and beliefs that created the experiences of our past. For if we keep summoning forth the same intent and beliefs of our past into the present moment, we are not laying the past to rest, but instead we are carrying around the baggage of a time period that has vanished. But when we attempt to let go of this baggage and change our lives, this does not sit well with those who are beholden to keeping the traditions of the past alive and with them, the myths they are framed in. In many cultures and families, the tradition of remaining in a marriage or a specific type of career, and not breaking tradition of any kind, is still rigidly upheld. The winds of change are upon us, however, as Baby Boomers are increasingly getting out of bad marriages at a rate that was once inconceivable.

In their published report titled, *The Gray Divorce Revolution: Rising Divorce Among Middle-aged and Older Adults, 1990-2010,* Susan Brown and I-Fen Lin, from the National Center for

*"The divorce rate among adults ages 50 and older doubled between 1990 and 2010."*

Family & Marriage Research at Bowling Green State University in Ohio, say that, "The divorce rate among adults ages 50 and older doubled between 1990 and 2010." The report also concluded that by 2010 25 percent of divorces were with couples over the age of 50.

Although these statistics and similar studies speak to a significant shift in how our generation is letting go of long-held belief systems, what they do not offer is the underlying cause behind such a break in tradition. It is one thing to believe it is time to break free from one myth and successfully do so. But if we remain oblivious to the underlying cause of all the myths, we will continue to be tied to the past, driving through life with a blind spot in our seemingly never-ending quest to feel loved and appreciated.

The intention of our parents and society to honor marriage is understandable. But binding people to ways of living that are not in alignment with a mutual quality of life is dysfunctional and unhealthy. Unfortunately, tens of millions of Baby Boomers learned this the hard way. This is why it is important to not sugarcoat our painful experiences from the past so we do not repeat them in the new life we are creating. Whatever we think we lost in our youth, we gained in the knowing that we deserve to live our best lives and love freely without restrictions. In short, we've learned to *Drive-Thru-Life and Make It Our Own®.*

## THE IDEA OF WE

Allan and I still remain in contact to this day. He is a good man and we had a good marriage. There was a beginning, a middle and an end. In our case, we broke our vow of, "until death do us part", as the marriage ended before either of us died. I thank him for sharing our youth and business years together. We accomplished a lot and I would never look upon our lives and regret any of those years.

Allan's encouragement was a huge factor in pursuing my life-long dream to be an actor. He produced the play, "Father's Day", for me so that I could perform the complex and emotionally rich role of Louise. This experience provided me the confidence to know I had the talent to carry a lead role. It was also during my marriage to Allan that my mother and I had the best stretch of our relationship. For better or worse, Allan and I are separate and independent with our own personal lives. Still there will always be a "We" *(you and me)* with me and Allan. The idea of the "We" is ingrained in me, etched into my soul and my past. "We" is woven into the fabric of my life, into the very design of who I am, how I live and how I came to be the way I am. "We" is woven into who I am in the present moment.

In his acclaimed book *The Four Agreements* author Don Miguel Ruiz writes that "95% of the beliefs we have stored in our minds are nothing but lies and we suffer because we believe all these lies." Like so many Baby Boomers who were groomed on the idea that we go to college, get married, have a family and live happily ever after, the reality of that fairy tale faltered along the way.

I wouldn't go so far as to say the way marriage was explained to us was a lie. I will say that few parents ever truly discussed the realities of what marriage was like with their children, during the era we grew up. It was a different time and for Boomers, we had to figure out what worked and what didn't on our own. This isn't necessarily a bad thing, but when you're raised on stories that tell you life is

184

supposed to be perfect if you follow the script, the reality of that script being completely rewritten without you knowing your role can be scary and utterly heartbreaking.

The power of surrendering to who we are and where we are in our lives becomes overwhelmingly obvious. What else is there to do but to accept this is my one and only moment of youthful exuberance? Anything else is a pipe dream that will always go up in smoke because we are looking into a world of shadows when we peer into our past, hoping for it to return in some manufactured glory. For this and many other reasons, I look upon my time with Allan as a prelude and preparation for the life of exuberance I live today. How can I not be grateful for that period of my life?

# Chapter 12

# ~ BORN UNDER A LUCKY STAR ~

*"Just beyond the trenches of struggle awaits your true*
*happiness."*
*Joanie Marx*

I am only a few yards from my mother's hospital room and I cannot take another step. All of these memories from our past coalesce into the present moment. We hear all the time about how people's lives flash before their eyes in a life and death moment. That's what is happening to me as I am facing the decision whether my mother lives or dies. While I'm not the one dying, it sure feels that way.

Needing to turn off the flashing imagery and quiet the inescapable chaos of the memories flooding my mind, I am compelled to find a place to sit before I collapse. After locating an empty chair, I sit down and take a few deep breaths. The hallway is filled with a mixture of noises and scurrying feet. It takes a moment, but I eventually center myself. In doing so, I realize the process of looking back on our life together is helpful but it is not going to erase my mother's current situation. It is at this time I am transported back to the day that ultimately led us here.

With clarity, in my concise adult business voice, the words march out of my mouth directly into the medical receptionist's face. "We have been waiting over an hour now for this ultrasound test. I told you when we checked in that my mother has a severe case of dementia. She is starting to get too tired and is going to become very difficult to handle."

The receptionist unsympathetically replies, "I told you we have to work her in. All the other people have appointments." Without missing a beat and completely undeterred, I fire back, "I know we don't have an appointment. That's why this is called an emergency." A standoff between us ensues. After a few tense seconds of silence the receptionist agrees to go find someone to help us

Finally, the ultrasound technician comes out to report we have to wait only 15-20 minutes more before she can do mother's test. By this time, it is after 5:00 pm and I'm wondering if there is even a doctor around to read the test results. I leave her sitting in the wheel chair to go to the restroom. I am washing my hands when it hits me, "Oh, my goodness, Mother is wearing a diaper." In all this commotion of getting to the emergency room and my focus on my mother's condition, I didn't think to ask the nursing home staff to give me fresh diapers. I think to myself, "I can't do this. I can't change my mother's diaper." I rush out of the restroom and return to my mother's side in the emergency waiting room.

"Ma, how are you?" She nods her head, "I'm fine. What are we doing here?" she asks. "We're at the hospital," I reply. "When you woke up this morning your knee was very swollen. We need to do an ultrasound test." She is perplexed, "I don't understand a word you said. I feel fine. I want to go home."

I knew if we didn't get in sooner than later this was going to happen. I do my best to reassure her that we need to do this test on her knee. She is having none of my explanations and this conversation repeats itself for several more minutes until, for a brief interlude, my mother realizes her knee is severely swollen. Thankfully, at that very instant we are called in for the ultrasound and my mother's attention is diverted.

188

## PLEASE, SOMEONE HELP ME

Getting my mother from the wheelchair to the examination table is no small task, for she is resisting the entire experience and has already forgotten what we're doing here. She is yelling at me, "Leave me alone! Stop pulling on me!"

I do my best to calm her down and explain that the ultrasound technician and I do not want her to fall and hurt herself. I reiterate what we're doing, but it only exacerbates the situation and my mother actually takes a swipe at the technician.

> *I then burst out with all my might, "Please, someone help me!" But no one hears my cries for help, because it is an internal scream.*

The ultrasound technician, who had kept us waiting for an hour and twenty minutes, starts to get nervous over this escalating scene between my mother and me. I look up at the technician, "I told you my mother would become hard to handle if we waited too long." She responds with the obvious, "I can't do this test if she doesn't get on the table."

"It's ok. I'll just hold her arms down." Mother is screaming louder at this point, "Get off of me! I'm getting

189

out of here!" I'm leaning over to keep her from moving but she starts pulling my hair. "Get off of me," she screams. This is turning out worse than I could have imagined and I am pleading, "Mother, please, let them do the test. It will be over very quickly."

"Let go of me! I hate you! Go to hell!" My only sense of awareness is to remain as calm as I can in the face of a situation that feels like it is about to become seriously out of hand. "No mother, I won't go away. I love you and I'm not letting go of your hands. Now just stop it. It will be over in a second. This doesn't even hurt."

There was a time when my mother could make my worst day all right by giving me a smile and a little encouragement. Sure, she was rigid in her beliefs and her expectations of me at times were unrealistic, but she was a beautiful, giving soul. This woman I am holding down for an ultrasound, who is screaming and shaming me, is not who my mother is. I find myself repeating in my head, "I want my mother back. I need to see her one more time."

There is a window of opportunity for the ultrasound test to begin as my mother stops fighting me. I train my eyes on the ultrasound screen. I see it, a black hole. It's a large blood clot. My heart sinks as the ultrasound technician confirms my worst fears, "It is positive."

As I wheel mother out of the exam room the technician says to me, "I feel so sorry for you." I don't acknowledge her words. We waited too long and mother is so tired. I'm already trying to hold my emotions together with what is becoming an unavoidable conclusion to my mother's deteriorating health. I have to remain focused and I'm wondering how will we make it through the rest of what surely will be a long night.

I wheel mother along the green linoleum floor, following the long red line to the double doors marked in red EMERGENCY. I lean in and whisper softly in my mother's ear, "Mother see how easy that was. We're fine. I love you and you're doing good."

I then burst out with all my might, "Please, someone help me!" But no one hears my cries for help, because it is an internal scream.

*A SACRED PHRASE*

Opening my eyes, I return to the present reality of sitting in the hospital hallway, outside my mother's room. I try to block out how she looked at me with such hate on her face that day during the ultrasound. The feeling transported me back to when I was a little girl. Only then I didn't have anyone to tell me "I feel so sorry for you." I love my mother with all my heart. No matter what she and I had been through, I never stopped loving her. But I could never control her behavior towards me. And I still can't.

We got through that night with the ultrasound tests and many other nearly unbearable experiences during her accelerated decline in health. As tough as those may have been to shoulder, they do not compare to the gravity of this moment. My focus returns to the one thing I remain resistant to let go of; the need to surrender my fear of not having any control over my mother's health. I may have the power to make a decision to end her life, but it is not the control I want. I did not ask for this. Or did I?

I get up from the chair, take a deep breath and inhale all of my fears and doubts. As I exhale, I am consciously aware that I am releasing decades of self-inflicted punishment for feeling unworthy and believing the decisions I make wouldn't measure up to my mother's expectations. I find an increasing sense of freedom to look further within and know that this decision to end my mother's life was my decision to make. There was no one to blame and no one to call for help. I was scared but at the same time there was no one else I would entrust to make this decision. It's all on me. I can do this.

Entering my mother's room I see her lying in the bed, her eyes closed. She peacefully sleeps completely unaware of what is being decided for her. I gently take hold of her hand. She feels my presence and touch, her eyes slowly opening. As she looks at me, I wonder if she even recognizes who I am. A slight smile begins to form and a glint in her eyes suggests that she does. Another memory washes over me, the force of this experience crashing down on me in my most vulnerable moment.

This time my mother sits on my bed, gently stroking my hair. I am sick and hoping that this wonderful nurturing side of her stays around longer than my illness. I glance up to her and she can see I am frightened by how sick I am feeling. She reassures me as only she can, "Don't be scared, Joan. Remember, my little girl, you were born under a lucky star. You're going to be feeling better in no time. Nothing terrible will ever hang around you very long."

I was born under a lucky star. It was not the first time I'd heard her say this to me, nor would it be the last. It became the foundation for my belief system and how I viewed myself in the world. For even then, as a little girl, I felt the magical essence and power of this sacred phrase. It is the one gift that my mother gave to me that has transcended all others. I always understood it to mean that if I put in the necessary work

*"Don't be scared, Joan. Remember, my little girl, you were born under a lucky star. You're going to be feeling better in no time. Nothing terrible will ever hang around you very long."*

and focus, everything will work out favorably. Although, things didn't always turn out as I had originally envisioned, my mother's conviction of its truth reverberated through my soul and kept me on course. It is a sacred belief and has been a compass for me to navigate through some of the toughest stretches of my life. It is my truth.

This sacred phrase of being born under a lucky star is what I am grasping hold of right now as I look down on my frail mother. I embrace the depth of its meaning, allowing the idea of it to provide a sense of stability and certainty in this unsettling moment. But isn't a moment like this why my mother instilled into me the meaning of being born under a lucky star?

I am trying so very hard to call upon the power of this phrase when I need it now more than ever. But the only thing I can think of is wanting my mother to read me one more story, to share one more creative piece of timely advice for how to handle this. Oh, the magical warm light of her attention. I craved that attention even if it was hand delivered to me at times as a gift in dualistic wrapping paper.

My smile dissipated as the memories of the past fade, giving way once again to the reality of this possibly being our last moment together. Truth be told, it wasn't lost upon me that in deciding whether I approve of killing her, I was in essence killing a huge part of myself. I realized this was not a fair approach, using the good and bad memories as a measuring stick for determining if I would make the decision to end my mother's life. Some were simply more joyous or more painful than others. In this desperate need to quiet the emotional storm swirling in me, I am reminded of one of the most painful aspects of my relationship with my mother - that I never had children of my own.

*A FAMILY OF MY OWN*

My mother is the primary reason I chose not to have a family of my own. I couldn't escape the idea of not having children being the worst decision I ever made. I'd often thought of having children, but the idea my mother would give them more attention than she gave me was too much to bear. There was always competition between us and it wasn't healthy. It wasn't something I asked for, but it was a reality I had to deal with. To compete for her attention had been the single hardest competition growing up. No way was I going to put myself or my child through that.

During my childbearing years, when I was married, it just so happened that my relationship with my mother had turned a miraculous corner. For nearly 12 years, we were enjoying the best stretch of our relationship ever. I surmised that by starting a family, all of that would have changed for the worst, or at least I thought at the time it would. I would have lost her attention and the joy of having children would have been lost with it.

Here I was, enjoying the relationship with my mother I had craved since I was a little girl. Finally, I had the respect and acknowledgement of my mother, who was my best friend. Why would I want to create a competitor for her attention? That was the last thing I wanted, as competitive scenarios like that would not be in anyone's best interest. Call it selfish, but I simply could not do that to myself, let alone to my unsuspecting children. This decision was not an easy one to face, for I was not immune to the teachings of society, that it was our job as women to be mothers. Now so many of my fellow Baby Boomers have had children and grandchildren. Being an only child and having to endure the ups and downs of isolation, I had a slightly different perspective of what it would mean to bring a child into this world.

I thought the decision to not have children was something I had gotten over, and here I was reliving that, along with everything else between my mother and me. All the experiences, real and imagined, had risen up one last time to be forgiven and surrendered. So here I am forgiving myself for thinking I had done something wrong and forgiving my mother for all those years I spent fighting to be seen, heard and acknowledged by her.

It's true, I had done my best to ignore the impact of these experiences, even though I was aware of them. When you are faced with what is an impossible to undo decision, the very act of avoiding our negative emotions gives them the power to control our lives. In the final moments of my time with my mother, there was no more room for any control issues. As author John Gray once said, "What you feel you can heal." And I was feeling everything from my experiences with her.

## *THE POWER OF BEING PRESENT*

When we listen to our feelings with compassion, the power our negative feelings have over us dissolves. We are able to respond to situations in a much more loving and respectful way. This is what I was doing that day in the hospital room with my mother, releasing what no longer served me. And I've been doing that every day since then.

I've come to know that I am not my feelings. Feelings change and the full spectrum of them, be they anger, sadness, fear, regret and love, are merely tools for us to utilize in our pursuit of being our authentic selves. When we spend our lives trying to appease others, namely our parents, we so very quickly lose sight of who we are. That is perhaps one of the greatest lessons I've learned from my mother. This takes me back to being born under a lucky star.

No matter what stories I'd told myself about my limitations or strengths growing up, I could always find my balance, my center, by remembering what my mother said all those years before, "Remember, my little girl, you were born under a lucky star. You're going to be feeling better in no time. Nothing terrible will ever hang around you very long." Feelings change and nothing terrible will last. Herein lies the power of being present in our lives.

To be present with my mother in this moment is as sobering as it is liberating. Never had I been so aware of my own life choices. I couldn't help but reflect on my journey and what this meant to the path that was ahead of me. I knew enough

*When we listen to our feelings with compassion, the power our negative feelings have over us dissolve.*

to realize that nothing would be as it once was, after my mother passes on. Then again, since her health started to decline, nothing in my life or hers remained the same. Here I was contemplating whether my mother is going to live or die, but it really wasn't about that as much as it was the quality of life that she had lived or would live. And that's just it. What is the definition of a quality life? How do we

199

measure something that we are not fully aware of ourselves, until it seems too late to make a difference? Is the quality of life we seek determined by one's past experiences? Or is this idea made up from false scenarios we project into an uncertain future that hasn't happened yet?

Sitting beside my mother, I felt myself beginning to break down as I realized the quality of life she has is nowhere near what she deserves. Tears streamed down my cheeks when I felt my mother's hand gently squeeze mine. I pulled myself together and for this briefest of moments, my mother looked at me the way a doting mother does to her child. There she was, my mother, my best friend. Mother Charming had returned.

For most of my adult life, I've never been one to shy away from letting my voice be heard. Right now, my voice was needed more than ever. What would I say to my mother when I opened my mouth? All those memories I'd been experiencing before entering her room and while I sat there, streamed across the photo album of my life. I began wondering how and where I had come to be who I am.

I quickly gathered my senses. I become aware of the true value and power of being present right then, for my mother wouldn't remain in this state of awareness for long. No more traipsing through the landscape of my past. This moment is as beautiful and as good as it will ever be. Leaning forward and whispering into her ear, I softly say, "You're going to be feeling better in no time, mother. Nothing terrible will ever hang around you long at all. I am here with you as I always will be. You and I were born under a lucky star. I love you."

# Chapter 13

# ~ NO CHEESE DOWN
# THAT HOLE ~

*"Thoughts are a prelude to action. You have to think*
*differently to behave differently."*
*Joanie Marx*

I am a Berkeley graduate. I can do this. And there is much to do. Get a job; get a better job. Get money; get more money. Buy things; buy more things. Start a business; grow the business. I want to be rich. I've always wanted to be rich. It was something that was instilled into me by watching others struggle and feeling if I could succeed financially I would be in control of my life. Beyond the money, the primary incentive for me to succeed financially was to earn the respect of my mother, and honor my father's love for me. Although he passed on way too early to see my eventual success, his role in my life never goes unnoticed.

While I worship and adore my mother, hanging on her every word, I leave myself vulnerable to never feeling good enough. I scurry forward, as always, consumed in a blaze of dogged determination to be rich and successful. I may have felt alone in a lot of things I did in life, but in this desire, I know I am not alone.

The pursuit of the American dream is the Baby Boomer mantra. It was, after all, an idea that revitalized the hopes of a nation after World War II and globally branded the era we were born into. This pursuit of a better life has proven to be as much of a cautionary tale as it has been an inspiration for those who have found the cheese they were seeking in the maze of life. But what about those people who were told to never deviate from focusing on a specific path, even though it is a path in the maze of life that will never produce the cheese they seek?

## THE STATUS QUO OF CHASING CHEESE

If a mouse does not find the cheese it is looking for in a particular passage, it simply turns around and without hesitation, resumes searching down another path in the maze. This process is repeated until the right path leads the mouse to where the cheese is located. People, however, are quite different in the pursuit of achieving their goals in the maze of life. Convinced they will find cheese on the path they were told to go down, most people will stay on that path searching for an outcome that will never materialize.

This painful and highly discouraging process of hoping for cheese, where there is none, isn't the exception to the rule. It is the status quo. Since this is the status quo, any attempt to point out the absurdity of remaining on a cheese less path is met with resistance by society, and most are shamed and blamed into remaining silent.

Like so many of my fellow Boomers, the idea of never giving up was drilled into my psyche. Follow the rules, respect your elders and do not question authority. This was told to me in many different ways, but the message was always clear. And who was it that told us to keep going down the path where there is no cheese? The very people we were told never to question.

It is no surprise, then, that Boomers are well known for remaining on a path, stubbornly refusing to budge even though there is clearly no cheese down the hole they have dug for themselves. And then, there are the anomalies. These are the people who somehow manage to manifest cheese where it was believed never to exist. Their efforts seem to support the idea success can to be found on every path and there is cheese down every hole we dig. When this happens, a new path in the maze emerges and a great many flock to it, eagerly digging their own holes in a desperate attempt to find their block of cheese. Some will find cheese, but eventually the hole will dry up and the path becomes yet another cautionary tale. This inevitable reality does not stop those who are convinced to stay on a path with no cheese. In fact, it actually reinforces their desire because they believe it's been done before and therefore, it will be done again.

> *Life is improvisational. It doesn't follow your script. Life would be easier if we accepted this.*

There are many different reactions for those who do not find cheese down the hole they were promised. Some demand the cheese be there. Others go so far as to expect that it be brought to them. The question is, why would seemingly intelligent adults regularly do this to themselves? There are, after all, many different paths in the maze of life that have an abundance of cheese down each particular hole. Still another question is, what kind of cheese are we really seeking, and what are we prepared to let go of in order to get it?

*CHASING SELF-ACCEPTANCE AND LOVE*

The idea of not giving up is so misunderstood that many in our generation have literally killed themselves and others in order to not be perceived as quitters. No one would accuse a mouse of giving up when it changes direction and ventures along a new path to find cheese elsewhere. Unlike mice, we are taught to stay in one place and never give up trying to succeed no matter the costs. Despite the reality of cheese never materializing, never giving up is the status quo because everyone does it. The real definition of giving up, however, is when we remain in one place too long, falsely believing the cheese we seek will magically appear, when it's clear it won't.

To do as the mouse does, which is astutely recognize a dead-end, turning around and returning to the search in another part of the maze, is not quitting. Unlike the mouse, however, people are confused by what they are searching for, which opens them up for all sorts of unfortunate experiences and unnecessary suffering. Whatever idea we ascribe to the meaning of the cheese, it is much deeper than money, a soul mate, or a highly sought after career achievement. The real prize of our pursuit for cheese is our belief that the path we're on will yield us love and self-acceptance from others, namely from the people who told us to go down a path where cheese is supposed to be.

Life is improvisational. It doesn't follow your script. Life would be easier if we accepted this. But for most of us, including myself, it's easier said than done. A mouse is relentless in a pursuit of a script that plays over in its little mind. It is a script that promises, "There is cheese down that path." It is this predictable script that drives the very purpose of the mouse, but the mouse does not get hung up on one specific path. That is not the script most Baby Boomers followed.

To understand what it is we're pursuing, let us consider that finding cheese is akin to wielding a magical device in front of our family and society, demanding we be given praise, acceptance and love for our great achievement. This is all part of the script. But what happens when the script changes? How quickly do we adapt, if we adapt at all?

While the answers may not always be the same for each person, my research for the book, coupled with my own experiences, have led me to identify a consistent set of reasons why Baby Boomers refuse to give up on the belief that the path they're on is the right one. They include, but are not limited to:

- Being told "the cheese would be down that hole" by someone they respected and trusted.
- Believing "the cheese would be down that hole" because they were diligent in following the instructions given to them, doing all that was asked and required of their efforts.
- They believe they are entitled to have the cheese down this promised hole.
- The belief that by waiting and then fuming, raging and demanding the cheese be there, it will miraculously appear.
- Believing that they have an infinite amount of time and energy to stand in one place and wait until the cheese materializes.

In the case of your average mouse there is no energy spent on why cheese is down any particular passage. It doesn't perceive the need to pursue the cheese for self-acceptance or associate its pursuit with love from other mice. If the mouse comes to a dead end, it doesn't throw a tantrum or blame other mice for the cheese not being there. Nor does the mouse demand other mice bring the cheese to him. When there is no cheese, the mouse turns around and refocuses its energy in a direction that produces the quickest return on the investment of its time and energy. This is to say that a mouse is impeccably proficient in not wasting its time or effort.

*ALL THE TIME IN THE WORLD*

In our youth we didn't accept the ideas of aging. Remaining forever young underscored our belief we could not be denied what was ours to have. Even in setbacks we found new ways of persevering. This was especially true when no cheese was discovered down the path we were traveling. We knew of people who discovered cheese down seemingly impossible paths. Anomalies existed and therefore, we knew it could be done. These anomalies reinforced the idea that all it took to manifest the illusive cheese was never giving up, regardless of how much energy and time it took. We Baby Boomers had an abundance of energy and time. Or so we thought.

As we begin to age, we see our life's finishing line on the horizon. Now, we know time is finite. Scarcity starts to look and feel very real as the reality of time and our capacity to manufacture the energy we once had in our physical youth diminish. If we believe we no longer have our youthful looks, or can summon the energy to find the cheese, there is a real danger of perceiving one's self as no longer useful to society. Depression, anger and anxiety settle in and from there it is a slippery slope into manifesting life's worst experiences. This is precisely where the media, advertising and entertainment industries step in and play off of the ideas of aging as a disease, reinforcing scarcity driven thoughts. If there was ever a status quo for us to disrupt, it is this one.

There is more creative energy within us than we have been led to believe. We need to say to ourselves, "there is no cheese down this hole" and proudly move on to another path until we find the hole with the cheese. Can we accept that we have time and energy in the present moment of our lives to do this? What if we rewrite the script we were given many years ago and accept we are worthy and good enough? If we did, would we be so willing to waste time and effort looking for something that isn't there and doesn't fit who we are now?

## THE BUSINESS MAGICIAN

Once Allan and I formed our own business, I found myself being the business magician. I assumed this new life role by calling upon my skills for solving problems in the nick

*We suffer because we don't accept where we are. Where we are, though, may be in need of a drastic change.*

of time. I became that anomaly who could make cheese *(solutions)* appear in places others couldn't. I was rewarded with looks of relief, delight and amazement from employees and customers. As I did with my mother, I routinely sought out Allan's approval for my efforts. What usually accompanied my accomplishments was a dampening chorus of "Now, Joan", from Allan.

Similar to the relentless pursuit mice undertake to find cheese, my end goal to be rich was not focused on a specific area of finding financial success, but rather making the most of the situation where it presented itself. Where I found myself getting tripped up was that I aligned my efforts and achievements to the recognition and love from others. For me, the cheese was not so much the financial success or even the solutions that helped generate our revenue. All of that served a goal that had once been hidden from my awareness, but was quickly becoming impossible to ignore.

My life went through a profound shift during the latter years of our marriage and owning the business. There came a point when I had to accept the approval I sought was very much the same as discovering there is no cheese down that hole. I could not associate my self-worth anymore to what my mother, Allan, or anyone else thought of me.

Accepting myself from within released me from feeling the need to keep heading down a path where I sought approval from everyone. Mind you, accepting this and putting it into action was not easy. There is no magical thinking and suddenly our future is different from our current life. By changing the intention of our journey, we change the path itself and that of our future. The question is, what is our intent and how willing are we to change course when it appears we are heading in the wrong direction?

*ACCEPTING WHERE WE ARE*

According to Buddha, we suffer because we don't accept where we are. Where we are, though, may be in need of a drastic change. Determining the change requires us to take a good, honest look inward. This took me a long while to completely grasp. For most of my life, I found it challenging to silence the extraneous noises amidst the flurry of activity surrounding me. By gifting myself a quiet space to understand what it is about my life that is in need of change, I was able to see where I was thinking through scarcity, when I thought I was operating through abundance.

Letting go of beliefs that no longer served me was as painful as living with them. The ideas of being a business magician now had to be applied to being a magician for my own life. It was very clear to me my future would be exactly the same as the life I was living unless I changed my current circumstances. I was troubled by a reoccurring question of how quickly the ripple effect of change would materialize into a form by which I could indisputably point to and say, "There, my life is different and it has changed for the better."

*If we're not fully aware of what is driving our desires, our fear of success and failure can derail our best laid plans and leave us scrambling for cheese that is not there.*

To answer that I knew I couldn't shy away from acknowledging a simple truth. I navigated my life with complicated and conflicting operating systems. This made it nearly impossible, at times, to determine what was in my best interest.

If we're not fully aware of what is driving our desires, our fear of success and failure can derail our best laid plans and leave us scrambling for cheese that is not there. It happens when we unknowingly anchor our desire for a better life to what others will think of us. This is the foundation of scarcity-based thinking. We see within ourselves something we lack and we set sail on a journey to find and accumulate what we believe will fill this void. If we are buying into the myth there is not enough happiness to go around, it is easy to get stuck in a pattern of dysfunctional behaviors that will never produce what we want.

When it came to chasing the cheese down the hole, for most of my adult life, if the cheese was not there, I would never accept it. I was told it would be here, I'd say to myself. I worked hard for it to be here and I sacrificed a lot in my efforts to find it. I'd prayed for it to be where it was supposed to be. I'm entitled to it. It took a while for me to realize that no matter what area of my life I did this, until I could come to terms with what would satisfy me, no amount of determination and focus to find the cheese would help.

# Chapter 14

## ~ THOUGHTS THAT SUSTAIN US ~

*"No one can help you accept change, experience grief, or move on from loss. You must do these for yourself."*

*Joanie Marx*

My mother was the youngest of seven children and the fifth surviving daughter. She always prided herself on being the seventh child of seven children, having seven letters in her first name and seven letters in her last name. She had no middle name. Always running to catch up and surpass her older four sisters, she poured her energy into learning and memorizing the primary school books for each grade, even before she stepped into that class. What captured her interest more than anything was how light fell on objects and illuminated them. It was this fascination and her creative gift for painting that offered her a sanctuary to express her inner joy.

While in high school, my mother received a scholarship to the Chicago Art Institute. She was a woman of enormous talent, but little drive to succeed in the traditional sense. She admired lovely things, but didn't feel a pressing need to own them. Neither money nor status concerned her. She loved my daddy and me and the people she allowed into her inner circle.

My mother's philosophy of life was shaped by her idea of perfectionism. For instance, her artwork lined the school hall walls for Parent's Night and other special events. Her parents would say, "That's nice," but never came to the school to see her creations. As a perfectionist, she had a hard time ever accepting a compliment. She rarely spoke about the lack of acknowledgment from her parents. But, it clearly affected her more than in the way she would later raise me. My mother had a quick mind, a keen sense of humor and a wonderful writing style. Because she never fully cleared out the pain from her parent's denying themselves the enjoyment of honoring her gifts, she was never comfortable fully embracing her own gifts or mine.

## THAT'S JUST LIFE

My mother raised me to hide where I was hurt by others. Never let them see where the arrows hit me. That was a huge obstacle to overcome as an actor, which requires vulnerability. As an actor I had to show where that arrow landed and how it affected my character. Maybe the

216

character I'm playing has to hide the full impact of the pain, but it is incumbent upon a good actor to reveal an emotional reaction that is truthful to the scene. Doing so provides the audience a view into the overall scope of the character's primary objective.

For example, if you are a cartoon, you can act like you're mortally wounded and then miraculously pull out the arrow and be on your way. In a real-life drama, no one is going to ignore the fact that they are mortally wounded. Reluctant to be vulnerable, amateur actors choose not to go to the place that is most real. This produces an inauthentic performance. We do not have to be actors to understand or apply the lesson here. We owe it to ourselves to stop making up a fake response that is outside the boundaries of who and what we are. When we allow ourselves to willingly release our fears, our real selves emerge and life becomes more exciting and enjoyable.

> *Love is more than feelings. It is a behavior.*

Our capacity to love ourselves is in the choices we make every moment. But no moment is more important than when we are asked to let go of expectations and know that we are in a safe place. This comes from surrendering the need to control our interactions with others, opening the doors for us to assume the behavior of genuine love. Love is more than feelings. It is a behavior.

Loving behavior nourishes our emotional well-being, creating feelings of warmth, pleasure, safety, stability and inner peace. As Baby Boomers, most of us grew up in a society that spoke of these feelings, but no one was ever really expected to experience them on a consistent basis. If we're not experiencing these regularly, what else must fill our time and experience, but the opposite of these qualities? To be raised in a world of contradictory belief systems is to accept a life of ups and downs as being normal. How many times have negative things happened to us or those we know, and the common response is, "Well, that's just life." If the experience of ups and downs were normal, how come they feel so abnormal? We go to great lengths to experience the feelings of love on a more consistent basis. At the same time, we are conditioned to expect the inconsistency of love, all but guaranteeing we are going to sabotage our own sense of joy.

Believing in the inconsistency of love, we unconsciously create scenarios that rob us of our happiness, reinforcing the myth that there isn't enough happiness and love to go around. If we don't get what we want, the belief of not being worthy of love is reinforced. This is the foundation of living in a scarcity-based mindset. If we have conflicting philosophies, each of which are rooted in varying degrees of scarcity, how can we ever come to see who we truly are? How can we accept that the Prince Charming we've sought after is inside of us? This is one of the primary questions that I found myself asking as I started writing this book. The journey of answering this took many unexpected turns, ultimately bringing me to the crossroads of my life. The journey of answering this took many unexpected turns, ultimately bringing me to the crossroads of my life.

It is inevitable that at some point in our lives the two polar opposite roads of wanting love and fearing love will intersect. This is our opportunity to stop running from ourselves and accept our shortcomings. No longer afraid to look into the mirror of our soul, we can see our imperfections from a place of acceptance. By embracing our authenticity, the on-again, off-again love affair we have had with life dissolves, magically opening us up to experience a life we deserve, rather than one we tolerate.

## OUR PHILOSOPHIES

We all operate under our own distinct philosophies. Our philosophies define our thoughts as much as they shape our lives. They can bring us to fulfillment and they can tear us apart, dragging us to the brink of total emotional breakdown. It is here, in the heart of our inner most fears, where our willingness to let go of what no longer serves us that the driving force behind our thoughts and actions is revealed.

All of us have a philosophy that directs our life's decisions. Most people rarely take the time to see that their philosophies, and thus, their thoughts, are at distinct odds with one another. Our psyche is a blinding

> *Most people rarely take the time to see that their philosophies, and thus, their thoughts, are at distinct odds with one another.*

kaleidoscope of contradictive philosophies competing for our full-time attention. Over our lifetime, these philosophies intrude into our experiences. They become so pervasive that it is not uncommon for us to forget who we are or how our behavior is impacting the lives of those we spend our time with.

220

It took me many years, and some very painful experiences, to realize my philosophy of getting through life was unknowingly rooted in guilt and shame. For me the guilt stemmed from thinking I did something wrong by never being able to fully satisfy my mother's expectations. The shame evolved from never feeling satisfied for what I did in my life. I am now aware of what used to drive my thoughts and because of this, I am better equipped to navigate life's challenges. During the research for this book, I also learned I am far from being alone in the experiences of living in guilt and shame.

Overlooking the contradictory nature of our thoughts and philosophies makes it increasingly difficult to pinpoint where the cause and solution are to the stresses we face in our lives. So often, we tend to perceive our problems as coming from an outside set of forces we cannot control. But, once we can see the distinct polarities and contradictions of our thoughts we have a much better chance at making lasting changes to our lives. To reconcile all of this we need to honestly look at where we seek validation outside of ourselves

In many respects, our generation was damned if we did and damned if we didn't. If we did what we wanted to do, we were labeled as being selfish. If we did what we were told by our parents and society, no matter what we accomplished, it was rarely good enough. Growing up, there were countless occasions when my mother would say how selfish I was for doing anything that wasn't aligned with her desires for me. When I followed her script for me and did as she wanted me to, I was praised. As quickly as I would receive her approval, I would find myself being critiqued for doing something that wasn't up to her standards. This was commonplace for many families of our era and still is. For some, this can be fuel to an unquenchable need to prove we are worthy. It is also where the seed of guilt and shame is planted, framing the philosophies and myths we were raised on.

## A BLURRED IDENTITY

In researching the book I've been asked why any of this is worth addressing and changing about ourselves at this stage of our lives? If we still find ourselves seeking for that long-lost sense of self-worth in other people and things, there is no better time than right now to de-clutter our ideas about life. Bringing our competing philosophies out of the darkness of our self-imposed denial, we can clearly see the thoughts that sustain us. This makes it so much easier to step into our authentic identity, instead of using a false sense of self to survive and hide ourselves within. Without being aware of who we truly are, our final years will be spent needlessly battling ideas and myths that have no bearing on who we have become, stealing away the quality of life we worked so hard to achieve.

As actors, we are taught to own the scene, but we are also taught to surrender the need to control the scene. Over the years, I learned the true value of surrendering by no longer managing my responses to manipulate my public image.

> *It is liberating to not know, except to know that you are surrendering to the uncontained beauty of the moment.*

Truthful acting is setting yourself up to be out of control, to be provoked, and emotionally triggered by your scene partner, honestly and without adding or changing that genuine response. Bad acting is re-directing the response from your partner and going to a safe/comfortable place instead of the actual response the words and scene partner evoke in you. An actor's prayer is answered when the lines ring true and the story grips the audience.

A great piece of acting is effortless and carries with it a spontaneous fluidity. It's fascinating to watch because you don't know the outcome or where it's going. It is liberating to not know, except to know that you are surrendering to the uncontained beauty of the moment. This does not mean you sit quietly and not participate. It means that you are not setting up restrictive rules and barriers to the outcome. In acting it is essential that the actor does not get ahead of himself and start acting the story's outcome before it actually occurs.

When I go into the audition for an acting role, I have to own that space. My energy changes the molecules in the room, so when I leave, what is left in the room is different because I was there. This happens when I do only what is required of me in that moment. Whether or not I get the role I'm auditioning for, I am not leaving my self-worth in the hands of someone else because I know who I am and what I am there to do. This is the essence of being truthful in the moment. The truth of who we really are is not easy to discern, though. Just when we think it seems our lives are defined, our world changes and the identity of who we thought we were becomes blurred. This is especially true when we look at the legacy of our generation through the distorted lens of society's perception about aging.

We've spent the better part of our lives moving at a breakneck pace to live our best lives. For a while our generation believed aging was conquerable and our thoughts about what constitutes a youthful life permeated the globe. Now that we've reached a point in life where society believes we are irrelevant, it becomes increasingly difficult not to perceive ourselves in much the same way. And so it is, once again, time for a change.

# Chapter 15

## ~ THE VANISHING ACT ~

*"95% of the beliefs we have stored in our minds are nothing but lies and we suffer because we believe all these lies."*
*Don Miguel Ruiz*

For my mother's 70th birthday I took her with me on a business trip to Hong Kong and Taiwan. During this time, I had the import-export business with my former husband, Allan. My mother was in good health and it was the first time I had her accompany me on an overseas trip.

During my appointments with our business contacts, my mother had a chance to go on some tours in Hong Kong and Taiwan. Each night she would happily recount her experiences and show me her drawings. Mother had taken with her a sketchbook and it was the first time I had seen her attempt any form of artwork since daddy's death six years earlier. For me, seeing her draw again was worth the trip.

*"What do they do with all the old people here? You don't see any."*

After our stay in Hong Kong, we flew to Taiwan. Our last night there, mother and I were joined for dinner by one of our key contacts in this region. Midway through the meal my mother inexplicably asked, "What do they do with all the old people here? You don't see any." I shot a quick glance toward our dinner companion, who was also surprised by the question my mother was asking. Intrigued, I asked her what she meant. My mother went on to explain that during our stay in Hong Kong and now in Taiwan, she encountered very few people who appeared to be over the age of 40. She said it was particularly obvious in the business sections of the two cities, which is where our hotels were located.

I casually looked around the restaurant we were in and I was struck by the realization that she was right. Few people appeared to be 40 years of age, let alone over 50. It was obvious my mother was the oldest person there and I couldn't help but wonder how uncomfortable she must have felt.

Upon returning to our room later that night, mother and I talked further about her observation of the lack of old people in the city business centers. She said she felt oddly out of place during her stay in Hong Kong and Taiwan and it wasn't because of her nationality. In her mind, even at 70 years of age, she considered herself young and vibrant. She couldn't understand how there were no other people who reflected her age. As I listened to her, I felt how visibly shaken she was by the absence of anyone over the age of 40. At the time, I have to admit I wasn't aware of the glaring absence of people her age. I was young and everyone I was interacting with for business was around my same age. I told my mother it never occurred to me there weren't many people in the business community beyond their mid-thirties. I reassured her that everyone her age in Hong Kong and Taiwan were probably enjoying a quiet and peaceful life away from the hustle and bustle of the city.

The following day on our way out of Taiwan, I keyed in on the disparity between people of my mother's generation and the overwhelming number of young people I saw. It wasn't until many years later, when I entered the world of acting, that the issue of society's disengagement with age came up for me again. When I started acting, I was in what some refer to as "no man's land." I wasn't young by Hollywood's standards, but I wasn't in the old category either. Thankfully, I was able to land some good roles to showcase my talent, but I soon realized talent alone is not enough.

It didn't take me long to realize the roles offered in Hollywood were based strictly on age. They say success is about who you know in this business, and to a degree that holds true. Honestly, it's more about your age than it is anything else. One's talent is perhaps the last thing that is of relevance. Everyone knows the extent of age discrimination in Hollywood, but rarely does anyone ever speak about it openly. Unfortunately, Hollywood is not alone in age discrimination.

Several years after I'd entered the acting business, the true nature of society's disengagement with aging came full circle as I began the process of writing this book. I was reminded of the experiences with my mother in Hong Kong and Taiwan, and I could now see how this was not an isolated incident. Little did I know then, but what my mother and I witnessed on the other side of the world was the effects of the 'Disengagement Theory'.

*THE DISENGAGEMENT THEORY*

In their 1961 book, *Growing Old,* social scientists Elaine Cumming and William Henry proposed their 'disengagement theory', which is based on the premise that "aging is an inevitable, mutual withdrawal or disengagement, resulting in decreased interaction between the aging person and others in the social system he belongs to." It is widely accepted this was the first theory of aging put forth by social scientists. Since its initial inception, the idea has been criticized for its universal application, all the while it remains universally applied by society, whereby aging adults are expected to disengage from social activity.

The 'disengagement theory' was framed around the idea that an aging population has no business in a social system that is youth orientated. In order to not feel ostracized, it was theorized that the older generation would voluntarily disengage

*The 'disengagement theory' was framed around the idea that an aging population has no business in a social system that is youth orientated.*

and disappear into the shadows of society's youthful bright lights. This may have made sense and held true for my parent's and grandparent's generation, but it is not who the Baby Boomer generation is.

On one level of thought, the 'disengagement theory' would be appropriate if someone is dealing with severe health issues, as my mother was late in her life. Extreme cases are not, however, what many social scientists, including the authors of the book *Growing Old*, based their theories on. Nor is it how our general society raised itself to separate the perceived older generation from the younger ones. It is not a stretch to say that this is a formula for the vanishing act of aging citizens of our world. While it may not appear to be the case on the surface, for we are always reminded to honor the elderly, at the core of 'the disengagement theory' there is a blatant lack of gratitude for those who have come before us. As we will come to see in the following pages of this chapter, and as it is woven into the theme of the book, if we are ungrateful for those who paved the path we now walk on it is impossible for us to know who we are, let alone be grateful for the beautiful lives we have right now.

By taking a glimpse into the last 50 years, it is easy to see how and where the 'disengagement theory' has been applied in all areas of society around the globe. This goes far beyond age discrimination lawsuits that have risen exponentially since the Baby Boomer generation passed the 55-year-old threshold. Our society has been programmed to perceive aging as a disease. The primary way this message is reinforced is through the false portrayals of aging by the media, advertising and entertainment industries.

The message delivered to society is carefully crafted, so as not to appear to uphold the idea that age is a disease, or that any one segment of the population is being discriminated against. Nevertheless, it is quite obvious what is occurring when you take into consideration the sheer size of the Baby Boomer generation, contrasted against the glaring absence of how positively our lives are portrayed in society the older we get. As disconcerting as all of this is, it becomes easier to grasp when we go beneath the surface level ideals and myths we were raised to live by and see the origins of our beliefs. For it is here, underneath the façade of honoring and respecting our elders, that the reality of how we see ourselves is revealed.

## A LACK OF GRATITUDE

What is perhaps most telling about the ongoing disengagement practices of society, and the industries that help reinforce them, is not necessarily what is said or shown in the media and advertising campaigns, but what isn't revealed. Silence is not golden when the golden years of our lives are predicated upon us silently disappearing. This is made clear to us by how blatantly absent Baby Boomers are from society's 24-7 news stories and advertisements about what constitutes a quality of life. We rarely see an accurate reflection of our true selves in anything.

When Boomers are shown in the media, it's usually a story or commercial that relies on negative based messaging. We are bombarded by messages and storylines about protecting ourselves from various threats and how to safeguard

> *"One of these lies that we believe and practice and reinforce is that getting older is getting uglier."*
>
> Oprah Winfrey

ourselves from what we're told we are losing as we age. It's seemingly impossible to escape the scarcity driven theme. Any genuine form of celebrating the older population is relegated to those rare milestones, which is always based on someone's age or a unique accomplishment.

When Oprah Winfrey recounted a conversation she had with Don Miguel Ruiz, author of, *The Four Agreements*, she addressed the idea of aging and gratitude by saying, "One of these lies that we believe and practice and reinforce is that getting older is getting uglier. We then judge ourselves and others, trying to hold on to the way we were."

Oprah went on to say, "I'm well aware that trying to stay fresh and current can be a challenge, especially if you live a lot of your life in public view. Of course, I want to look my best. I want to feel strong and vibrant. But, I know for sure that the pathway to your best life isn't the route of denial. It's owning every moment. Staking a claim in right now. And, with gratitude, embracing the age you are."

One of the biggest revelations for me in writing this book was seeing the absence of gratitude in our generation. It's not to suggest Baby Boomers are not grateful, for we are one of the most giving generations that have ever lived. When we look past the gift giving and even the joy many of us experience in our lives, we begin to more fully grasp the not-so-silent suffering those in the aging population go through, as their presence is unceremoniously phased out of society. To break the myths of aging and untangle the web the 'disengagement theory' has woven into our world, we will need to journey into one of the most significant and turbulent periods of modern history, which is the generational warfare that played out during the 1960's and early 1970's. Here, we can see more clearly the role this 'disengagement theory' and the lack of acknowledgment and gratitude has played in society's development and the impact this had on Baby Boomers.

234

## A PLACE TO BE OF VALUE

What caused generational warfare between Baby Boomers and the two generations that preceded us is the very same thing that continues to uphold the 'disengagement theory' in today's world. It is a lack of genuine gratitude.

Like so many other Boomers, I rarely approached my life from a point of gratitude because I was always focusing on what wasn't working. What is working well, I surmised, didn't need to take up my time or attention. My energy and focus was placed on problems, leaving me little time to be grateful for what was going well. This is not an exception to the rule for our generation. Our parents and grandparents, who had come out of two very painful and scarcity-driven eras, raised us on the idea of the world being a scary place and full of problems. As a result, our self-worth was rooted in how well we could solve problems, not on how grateful we were for what went right.

From World War I, through the Great Depression and onto World War II, people didn't have time to be grateful. They were too busy trying to survive. Problems were so big that even when one or more dire circumstances were overcome, no one had time to celebrate the victory. With one problem down there were another two-dozen or more to take its place. Our generation was born from this era and we were raised to see problems everywhere. In many cases, we were provided little information on the true nature of the problems, let alone how to enjoy the victories when we achieved them. The result of this was that most of our generation found themselves in a constant mode of survival without even realizing what had brought us there.

As we have covered in various parts of the book, the idea of vulnerability and expressing gratitude was perceived by many of our parents and grandparents as a sign of weakness. You cannot show people your emotions or you will be taken advantage of. However, our generation saw things differently. It may have taken us on a long and winding road, fraught with perilous twists and turns, but eventually we came to a profound realization: vulnerability symbolizes our strength and gratitude is the key that opens our heart to the beauty of life.

It took me up to the point of writing this book to fully grasp this. Instinctively, though, I began to understand how important it is to express gratitude, and honor those who came before me. This hit home for me after my father passed away. Daddy was gone and I cannot put into words the profound impact this had on both my mother and me. Without having a clue what the 'disengagement theory' was or pondering the idea of gratitude, following the passing of my father I brought my mother into my world on a level we had never previously engaged before. I provided her a space in my import-export company, which offered her talents as an artist and writer to be of value. She had a place to be appreciated during a time in her life when everything she once knew had seemingly vanished.

The relationship with my mother improved by leaps and bounds during this period of our lives. Having her there by my side allowed my mother to see where her contributions were valuable to the company and it reinforced the value of our love and admiration for each other. In no way was my mother discarded because of her age. She was not disengaged from my life, or I from hers. This, however, was not how our generation and our parents saw each other earlier in life.

## GENERATIONAL WARFARE

The vanishing act between generations isn't just about an aging population disappearing from sight as much as it is about acknowledgement, gratitude and what people perceive as their self-worth. Our parents and grandparents bought into a reverse idea of disengagement where anyone

*Our increasing desire to be seen and heard, coupled with a new way of looking at ourselves and the world, was perceived as disrupting the status quo.*

younger than themselves, particularly their own children, were unapologetically ignored and dismissed. Rarely acknowledged and our self-worth constantly called into doubt, when this mode of behavior carries over into adulthood there is undoubtedly going to be high-levels of tension, particularly at the crossroads of life, whereby the older generation refuses to hand over the keys to the kingdom to the younger one. Eventually, the younger generation is going to rise up and claim what they rightfully believe is being held back from them. In contrast, the older generation will fight tooth and nail to preserve the status quo. It was here, our generational battle cry that you cannot trust anyone over the age of 30, came into existence.

The emerging industries of that era, most of whom targeted a youthful demographic, took full advantage of this ever widening rift. They had a vested interest in helping escalate this division, making sure that by playing both sides there were huge profits to be made by both the winners and losers. And the younger version of our selves played right into the stories and campaigns being fed to us. Having been relegated as obsolete in our own homes for so many years, it felt wonderful to be acknowledged, whether it was from our own peers or from a product, music, movies and fictional character we related to. Our increasing desire to be seen and heard, coupled with a new way of looking at ourselves and the world, was perceived as disrupting the status quo. This, as much as anything, prompted the establishment to fight back.

During those tumultuous years in the late 1960's and early 70's, the lines between our generation and the establishment of the time were drawn. We had the youthful exuberance and naïveté to fight for what we believed in. Going to the University of California, Berkeley, during this time, it was impossible not to participate in the protests and rallies that were omnipresent in that region of California. The energy was contagious and to see first-hand, the ever-widening gulf between the young and old was as jarring as

239

it was invigorating to think we could make a difference in closing the divide.

Due to our generation's size and the advancements in technology, our presence was changing the landscape of the world, but it wasn't necessarily making peace with the establishment. The more we made our presence known and felt, the establishment pushed back harder than anyone believed they would. For a while, many youth of that era stood their ground and fought to the bitter end. But for most of us who were old enough at that time to make a difference, it became clear the further we rebelled, the less likely we were going to enjoy a quality life on the terms we wanted.

It didn't take long for Baby Boomers to bask in the glow of being the predominant audience for a vast array of products and services, many of them never before seen. The idea of continuing to fight the establishment's ideology waned in favor of indulging in what the establishment seemed to offer in its distorted brand of gratitude and acknowledgement. This pivotal moment in time marked the first vanishing act of the Baby Boomer generation. Our voice and creative energy stopped being used to change the world in one way and was redirected into another area that forever altered how our world views itself. The age of consumerism was in full swing and we were the driving force behind it.

## NOT A NEW MESSAGE

As the generational war we had been engaged in for several years came to an end, the middle and latter part of the 1970's helped usher in the age of decadence and excess, which ebbed and flowed during the 80's and 90's. These were our peak earning years and our accomplishments appeared to justify our desire to chase outside fulfilment rather than keep fighting an ideological war. What's important to state here is that the underlining premise of that war, which was to be seen and heard, never went away. It has come full circle as our generation is now at the age many of our parents or grandparents were during the revolution of the 60's and 70's.

The type of messaging we see today for Baby Boomers did not start when we reached the age we are now. As evidenced during my trip many years ago to Hong Kong and Taiwan, and going as far back as when our generation was growing up, we were influenced by the 'disengagement theory' even if we'd never heard of the term. Those who were aging, as we went through our youth, were deemed unsexy, obsolete and were largely ignored as consumers. We

241

didn't care so much how they were treated because we were the younger audience. The media, advertising and entertainment industries were shining their spotlight on us at the expense of a population whose disdain for our generation was growing as much as our distrust of them was deepening. Something had to give and it did.

For nearly 30 years, we were the predominant driving force of consumerism. We become the establishment and in today's world it would look as if we outstayed our welcome. So, the question isn't whether Baby Boomers will be ignored like our parents and grandparents. This would seem obvious. The question now is, how does a generation who redefined the idea of youth and sex appeal, change society's perception that aging is not as unsexy as we once said it was?

The pervading thought in Hollywood and on Madison Avenue is that the 55 and older crowd are not sleek and sexy. This is reinforced in the media where stories, studies and statistics about aging seem to prove what is being sold is an accurate reflection of our current reality. As an actress in the entertainment industry, I can honestly say what is being shown to the world about people from my generation is far from accurate. There is a pervading myth that the only way to properly market to and communicate with Baby Boomers will scare away the youthful demographic these companies are much more interested in. The younger generation is raised on the belief that an older generation is obsolete and worst of all, symbolizes death. Sound familiar to what we were raised to believe when we were growing up?

Today's youth are being programmed to perceive Baby Boomers not much differently than how we saw the older generation all those years ago. There is an unspoken belief that the further away the young can stay from the old, the better. Clearly, this is not a new message.

## WE'RE NOT GOING TO ROLL OVER

A lack of gratitude for what each generation brings to society will only serve to keep upholding unnecessary struggles. The separation of the young from the old is something that has been driven into the psyche of society for nearly as long as Baby Boomers have been alive. The realities of the world we're now in, is that these stories and myths of an aging population vanishing quietly into the night are not in alignment with who we are. As one of the more celebrated Baby Boomers, Cher, once remarked in an interview, "This is the first generation that said, 'We're not going to roll over and play dead because we're a certain age.' It's like saying to

243

the Rolling Stones, 'OK, you've had your time in the sun. Now go put on some plaid shorts and play golf.'"

It is very easy to point to outside entities such as the media, advertising and entertainment industries as the culprits in how our world perceives itself. Certainly these may be the primary purveyors of society's belief systems, but they are ultimately nothing more than an outward reflection of our own inner belief about ourselves. As hard as it may be to look in the mirror, there is no way we can have our voice properly heard until the Baby Boomer generation accepts responsibility for cultivating a super-sized lifestyle that never really lived up to the hype we extended to it.

Considering that we're unquestionably the largest segment of the population, with an estimated $2.3 trillion dollars of disposable income, it shouldn't be too difficult to have our voice heard. So, why are we buying into disengagement practices we have been fed over 50 years and acting as if we cannot change what we helped create? Could it be that despite our generation's size and all that we have done to change the world during our lifetime, we are still burdened by the myth of being shamed and blamed for disrupting the status quo? What if we rediscovered who we are and in doing so, remembered just how powerful of a voice we really have? And what if, after all these years of pretending we're someone we are not, that we realize we are the status quo and the only ones stopping us from changing it is ourselves?

## A REAL EYE OPENER

Many of our generation have enjoyed a significantly higher quality of life than any group our age before us. Clearly, not everyone buys into the myths we've discussed in this book. But, what about the next wave of people who will soon find themselves at the age we are now? How will they see themselves portrayed in society? No matter how well off many Boomers have been, we have a responsibility to make a difference in the world in a way that puts to rest these myths about scarcity, love and aging. If not us, who? If not in our lifetime, when?

It's one thing to embrace our youth in the present moment, but could we change the world as we once set out to do when we were physically younger? Is it even worth doing at this stage of our life? It is when we consider just how pervasive age discrimination is, in all of its forms, and the impact the 'disengagement theory' has on America and around the world. Let's remember that age discrimination, in whatever ways and means it rears its ugly head, is about removing the aging population from mainstream society. This is the result of a lack of gratitude.

All of this reminds me of how oblivious I was about the vanishing act of the aging population when I was younger. My mother asking what happened to all the old people during our trip to Hong Kong and Taiwan was a real eye opener for me. Nothing, though, could prepare me for what I would come to see as I entered the world of acting and eventually becoming a Baby Boomer Advocate. My experiences have shown me that when we open our eyes to what is really happening, we also open our heart to the realities of how we treat others and ourselves.

> *If we do not use our collective voice to correct the various forms of age discrimination in our lifetime, how will anyone of us be able to look in the mirror and see who we truly are, let alone say we are living the best life we can?*

When we look across the landscape of our lives it becomes clear the 'disengagement theory' proposed by social scientists Elaine Cumming and William Henry doesn't hold up to the reality of the lives we are passionately living in today's world. The more people and the companies they work for realize this, the easier it will be for them to remain profitable by crafting an emotionally relevant message that genuinely relates to and resonates with the one audience that has the capacity to keep their brands from vanishing, which are Baby Boomers.

We cannot afford to overlook the truth that our generation helped teach the myth of aging to those who are now in charge of decisions for the brand of messaging that is coming through the media, advertising and entertainment outlets. With what we now know there are no excuses for why our generation or future generations should continue to be subjected to disengagement practices based on the falsehood that aging is a disease. If we do not use our collective voice to correct the various forms of age discrimination in our lifetime, how will anyone of us be able to look in the mirror and see who we truly are, let alone say we are living the best life we can?

This is why it is more important than ever to see where we misunderstood the power of our youth. In doing so, we can gift ourselves the space and time to reclaim a youthful voice that appeared to have vanished by applying the power of gratitude when and where it matters most. For it will be in our genuine appreciation for the life we lived that other generations will learn the true value of honoring those who came before them. Is there really a better legacy and gift we can give to the world than this?

# Chapter 16

# ~ MIRROR, MIRROR ~

*"Beautiful young people are accidents of nature. But beautiful old people are works of art."*
*Eleanor Roosevelt*

Am I who I see in the mirror? Now heavier than I have ever been, I am barely hanging on to the young cute self I have always believed myself to be. For a long time I have lived with what I now call the opposite of anorexia. I was getting heavier but I always thought I was the exact same weight I had always been. In my eyes the reflection in the mirror was my firm lean body of long ago.

So dear mirror, since I am neither as young nor as thin as I've always been, please do tell me how can I go out and seek a new life? What shall I use to capture the attention of others? I can't use my physical youth, as it is long gone. I can't call upon the middle years between youth and maturity, nor can I even rely on my current partner to remember me as I was then. Those who

> *"Time and tide wait for no man."*
>
> *Geoffrey Chaucer*

have come into my life in the last 20 years have no frame of reference of my younger self, for they only see what the mirror of today shows.

So now what? What will lure people into my world? What will entice them to stop and get to know me? I stand there before the image in the mirror of today, which is telling me to face the reality of my life and to own my advocacy slogan, *Drive Thru – Make it Your Own®*. I am compelled to change course, stop worrying, and drive down the "Reality Highway" to real places, real events and interact with real people.

In my conversations with other Baby Boomers, particularly women, I have come to know I am not alone in this internal dialogue between my internal self and the version of myself I see in the mirror. If we are lucky enough to live a long life, we will age. As English poet Geoffrey Chaucer once said, "Time and tide wait for no man." We all know this instinctively, but there is this innate resistance in facing and overcoming our fear of aging. How do we break the myths of our upbringing and fully inhabit each phase of our lives? One way is by using our life force to win the game of life by staying in the game and enjoying it. I have found when I relinquished my ideas about what I think I should physically look like at this age, things became easier. If I was going to step into the youthful exuberance of my present life I needed to honor who I am right now. The vision of my younger self, judged against the reality of what I look like now had to be let go. There was no more fooling myself into thinking my physical looks were the same as they used to be. Nor could I rely on the idea that some magical potion or cosmetic procedure would drastically turn back the clock.

Having a little cosmetic work done here and there to look the best for our age can be a beautiful experience. In our attempt to manipulate our outer and inner perceptions of beauty, we lose sight of what constitutes a healthy, quality life. For those who can financially afford procedures and are in good mental and physical health, I believe we owe it to ourselves to take advantage of what is available to us for cosmetic enhancements. Our expectations of what plastic surgery and cosmetics can do for us, however, should be realistic and age appropriate. The question we have to ask ourselves, then, is can we enjoy where we are at this age, if we are continuously attempting to reverse what is a natural process of life?

*FIREBALL OF ENERGY*

I am not ashamed to admit there are still moments when I catch myself wondering, "Where did that slim, petite fireball of energy go?" By fireball of energy, I am not simply referring to my 20's or 30's. When many Baby Boomers were planning their retirement, I was just getting started with a new career as an actress. Focused on making my mark, and doing what my heart had desired since I was a little girl, I paid absolutely no attention to what the outside world said a woman of my age should be doing. And I was not fixated on any physical changes taking place due to age.

It wasn't that I lived in denial, but I have always operated with a strong, positive inner perception of myself. A lot of this came from always remembering my mother's most powerful declaration, "Joan, you were born under a lucky star." This carried me through many battles of self-doubt I had. Although there were moments of inner turmoil I simply didn't swim in those shallow waters long.

During this renaissance period of my life, my mother's rapidly deteriorating health was consuming a good portion of my thoughts, energy and time. Despite the toll my mother's condition was taking on me, coupled with the

challenging emotions that lingered from my divorce, I was more vibrant and creative than ever. My overall confidence had never been stronger and I outworked, outhustled and outsmarted people half my age. And then, without any fanfare or warning, I felt myself starting to slow down.

The desire to be active, to feel sexy and achieve my goals were still there. But my energy level and even my own outward appearance were out of alignment with how I was still perceiving myself. This had absolutely nothing to do with what the outside world was saying about women my age. Up to that point I wasn't even fully aware of just how disengaged the world was with an aging population, nor had I begun conceptualizing the myths of the Baby Boomer generation. But I was aware of age discrimination in Hollywood. What actress over 35 isn't? I just didn't buy into it because, again, I saw myself not as I was perceived by others, but as I chose to perceive myself. Soon, I would come to realize that many of the challenges I was facing and those being addressed by my friends and fellow Baby Boomers, had less to do with our actual age than it did with how the world was raised to perceive aging.

## IS GETTING OLDER GETTING UGLIER?

There comes a point for all of us when the past catches up to the present and our understanding of the future and our place in it irrevocably changes. Although this happens differently for each of us, it always arrives in ways no one else can foresee. For me, it was navigating my mother's illness. That experience opened my eyes and crushed my heart. It would be several years later before I came to appreciate the true beauty of the relationship with my mother and the correlation this had on the way Baby Boomers were raised to see themselves.

> *There comes a point for all of us when the past catches up to the present and our understanding of the future and our place in it irrevocably changes.*

The stories we've been raised on, that aging is not sleek and sexy, has had disastrous effects on our generation, particularly women. I am more aware today than ever that not everyone believes they were born under a lucky star. I am quite fortunate that my mother's belief on aging rubbed off on me. I remember her commenting to me how she felt her 50's and 60's were her best years. My mother didn't have

an "age gauge" as many other women did. I can now see how this helped me enter the acting industry at a time when so many of my contemporaries were either looking for ways to regain their youthful appearance or had given up on their self-worth, settling in for a life less than what they deserved.

It's not easy to believe in one's self when everywhere you look you're being reminded of how physically flawed you are. No matter how strong willed or self-confident one may be, we cannot escape the reality that the world judges its inhabitants based on outward appearance as much as anything. It could be said that in our quest to be accepted and find our symbolic Prince Charming, we are not so much comparing ourselves to a younger version of who we used to be, but instead we are blindly chasing what society deems to be the current definition of sleek and sexy.

The advertisements we were influenced by during the late 1980's and 1990's were packaged with slick, inspiring images and the messages were told through motivational stories that reinforced our drive to live life to the fullest. The infamous line about "40's are the new 20's" and "50's are the new 30's" were commonplace. For a while the idea of thinking we were younger sounded good as we looked for new ways to hold onto the idea of what being sexy and

youthful really meant. And then, one day, we woke up and those days were in the rearview mirror along with everything else.

Our physical youth may no longer be with us but we still have the present moment of our lives, which are pretty good, right? Not if society has anything to say about it we don't. Over the last 20 years the sophistication of editing images, through Photoshopping and airbrushing, has become an art form. This has shifted society's perception of themselves in ways that are anything but positive. Not even the models in real life look as good as they do on magazine covers.

In an interview for Good Housekeeping, Oscar winning actress Sally Field talked about how her love and joy for the work she does outweighs the desire to artificially change her outward appearance. She said, "I don't want to look old and worn, but what can you do? My real focus is being an actor. I care more about having the opportunity to play roles that I haven't played than I care if my neck looks like someone's bedroom curtains."

## GAIN OR RECLAIM

Another well-known actress and advocate for inner beauty, Oprah Winfrey, once said, "One of the lies that we believe, practice and reinforce is that getting older is getting uglier. We then judge ourselves and others, trying to hold on to the way we were."

Perhaps we always believed we were ugly, which accounts for how catering to being sleek and sexy become a multi-billion dollar industry during our

*Cosmetic procedures on people over the age of 65 have increased 352% since 1997.*

generation. One industry that has benefited as much as any from Boomers seeking to reconstruct our outer appearance is cosmetic surgery. There are numerous studies that have tracked the exponential growth of this industry over the years. Global Industry Analysts, a leading market research firm, projected back in 2011 that Baby Boomers "seeking to keep the dreaded signs of aging at bay," will be the primary catalysts for growing the anti-aging market in North America to an estimated $114 billion in revenue by 2015.

These financial projections are reinforced by studies conducted by the American Society for Aesthetic Plastic Surgery, which said cosmetic procedures on people over the age of 65 have increased 352% since 1997! Another study sponsored by the American Society of Plastic Surgeons estimated approximately 3.3 million women and men over 55 years old had some form of cosmetic surgery in 2013.

In our high-school years and even well into adulthood, the popular people were always the prettiest. All that mattered were their looks, and their personalities and private lives were secondary. From society's perception, the better looking you were the more respect and admiration you received. The risk of chasing the admiration of other people's opinions can and often will carry risks that go beyond just the physical. When we only hang our hat on our looks, the struggle to gain an edge on aging or even to reclaim our youthful appearance can become unbearable. This produces an enormous strain on people who approach plastic surgery with unrealistic expectations without recognizing that aging affects everyone and no amount of cosmetic enhancements last forever.

Over the years, the cosmetic surgery industry has had to overcome the negative publicity of unscrupulous doctors who are more than willing to accommodate the wishes of any patient, no matter what the procedure risk may be or limited positive outcome is. A lot of this has changed as a significant shift in the number of doctors, who have become much more attuned to the patient's well-being, and thus will now only perform cosmetic surgeries when the intent of the patient is both emotionally and physically sensible.

Dr. Darrick Antell, MD, a plastic surgeon and an assistant clinical professor of surgery at Columbia University in New York City acknowledges the state of health Baby Boomers are in and how this affects their choices for cosmetic procedures. He is quoted as saying, "The Baby Boomer generation has taken significantly better care of themselves. They work out regularly and watch their diet, but inevitably, the aging process catches up with them. They want the external appearance to match what they are on the inside."

There is a lot to be gained by various types of procedures that fall into the category of obtaining an enhancement on a long desired physical attribute. The impact on someone's personal sense of self-worth can do wonders. These positive life-altering changes do go a long way to improving one's overall quality of life. And herein lies the benefits of a sensible and well-adjusted approach to anti-aging efforts that plastic surgeon, Mary Lee Peters, MD., revealed in a recent article, when she said, "Boomers want to stay active, relevant, and engaged with society in important ways. Their outlook on life is to do what they can to enjoy the years they have left."

## *NOT GOOD ENOUGH*

Whether it came from our parents, spouse, friends, the workplace or the media stories that influenced us, the message coming back was always the same. If we were not satisfied with our life we must try harder. Never give up, no matter how painful the journey may be. It didn't matter how it was said; the message was clear. To be loved and accepted we had to suffer first. The idea of being good enough to live a quality life without pain was sheer fantasy. Based on negative perceptions being projected on us, if we wanted to be acknowledged we had to keep making adjustments to who we were, which meant we subjected ourselves to abuse for believing we were never good enough. Nowhere was this more apparent than the enormous effort placed on how we physically looked.

For many of our generation the need to keep up appearances was directly related to our survival in modern society. So is it any surprise that our bodies became our enemy? Our generation began pushing themselves through extreme diet programs and fitness regimes in the late 70's and well into the modern era. Waist sizes shrank and weight loss became one of the most important factors for living a quality life. And yet it still wasn't enough. Thus, cosmetic surgery became the next frontier of the anti-aging movement. No matter how much money we made and regardless of how we looked at ourselves, it never seemed to be good enough.

At various intervals of life we may have gained some sense of self-worth for achieving a major goal, but those joyous and celebratory moments were always short-lived, because once we looked in the mirror we either saw ourselves as sleek

> *Chasing after physical appearances for ourselves, based on what society tells us defines beauty, is not the answer to creating positive, long lasting change.*

and sexy, or we didn't. And if we did see ourselves as looking great, there was little time to enjoy what we had worked so hard for as the fear of losing our sleek and sexy body was omnipresent. As we covered in the previous chapter, we lived in a world where gratitude was absent because our focus was on the problems of our lives and not what was going well. Therefore, even on those rare occasions where we were actually pleased with our physical looks, it wasn't enough.

Never gifting ourselves the time to really enjoy the fruits of our labor we kept working tirelessly to fill that void for the acknowledgement, love and admiration we believed would come our way. When it didn't arrive, we just kept trying harder. Unaware of what was causing our inner turmoil, many from our generation were led to chase the illusion of money, facelifts and Prince Charming as a way to feel special. The question we have to ask ourselves, then, is when does the idea of looking for love in all the wrong places end? It doesn't. When we physically leave this planet, the myths about aging and scarcity will continue for the next generation to figure out. That is, of course, unless we do something about it while we still can.

Chasing after physical appearances for ourselves, based on what society tells us defines beauty, is not the answer to creating positive, long lasting change. If we are going to reinvent who we are, and break the seven myths, it means

262

we are going to have to look at where we fell for false ideas of beauty and self-worth during our younger years. Despite how much fun we may think we're having now, there are underlining beliefs about life that permeate our thoughts. We were raised and conditioned that no matter how good we had it, it was never enough. So, here we are in what could be said the best years of our lives, where millions of Baby Boomers are more active, livelier and far more secure financially than previous generations our age. Yet so many of us are not satisfied as our generation grapples with the reality of being discarded to a life of quiet desperation.

## SAFETY, COMFORT AND LOVE

It's one thing to pinpoint where some of our life's discomforts come from, but unless we burst the false idea that we are not good enough, we won't see where our need to be accepted and loved has fallen short. Therefore, when we look back over the last 20 to 30 years it's easy to identify where we chased the symbolic idea of Prince Charming, particularly from a physical standpoint. The evidence of this isn't just in our own individual lives as much as it can be clearly seen in the billion dollar industries that have been birthed through our generation's desire to find safety, comfort and love outside of the only place they exist.

263

The idea that we are not good enough is clearly one of the most debilitating beliefs of our generation. If we're not careful we can be sucked into a belief that our past is so much better than our present. We see this with anti-aging products as well as the diet and even nostalgia industry, the latter of which has thus far exclusively catered to Boomers. Our past is given a glossy makeover and the sights, sounds and ideas of a so-called happier, carefree time is blasted into our psyche. This alone has taken a great many down a dark and perilous path into all sorts of experiences to feel safe, comforted and loved.

There comes a point for all women and men, regardless of our generation, when we can no longer rely on ideas of physical youth any more than we can call upon cosmetic enhancements to communicate who we think we are, or what we believe the world will accept from us. There will arrive an inevitable point in all of our lives when the only thing that matters is our authenticity. This can only come from whom we accept as our truest self in the moment, which requires us to change our perspective about life. Not in the past or the future but right now.

*I LOVE YOU*

There was a pivotal moment for me during the writing of the book when I was explaining some of my experiences to Sue, my dear friend and college roommate. Sue is a brilliant writer and I valued her take on what I was going through. We talked about the inner dialogue we have with ourselves and the challenges of loving the person we see in the mirror. After one of our more poignant conversations she sent me the following:

"Being real and at ease with who we are gives all those around us permission to be the same. I stand in front of the mirror each day and look my aging reflection in the eyes and say 'I love you.' On the day you know that is true, you will see it reflected back to you. From that knowing, your inner beauty will shine forth. I believe people respond to and admire physical beauty, but they are irresistibly attracted to inner beauty."

Reading Sue's eloquent words remind me to embrace the unexpected joy of being in the journey of now. The process of gently reassessing the vision of my life, as it was reflected in the mirror, became a more joyous experience. The moment then arrived when I was compelled to leap into the unknown by asking myself, "Now what? How do I avoid the fade-out, loss of energy and focus needed to attain my Life Charming"?

Summoning the strength and courage of facing this question head on, a new way of perceiving what was around me began to profoundly shift my reality. I can see the finish line of my life, albeit on a distant horizon. By expressing a newfound sense of gratitude for what each new day offers me, my life is provided a unique sense of urgency. Unlike the past, this does not carry the burdens of who I used to think I needed to be in order to feel I was worthy. For the first time in my life I can look in the mirror, say, "I love you" and not only feel it, but know that I accept it.

# Chapter 17

# ~ VIRGINS NO MORE ~

*"You know you're getting old when you buy a sexy sheer nightgown and don't know anyone who can see through it."*
*Joan Rivers*

Carrying my books to and from school each day, I pass Trudy, the manager for the Tip-Top Trailer Park. She stands tall in her black leather spike heels, wearing oversized gold earrings, bright red lipstick and her hair large enough to house more than one beehive. Her larger- than-life-sized breasts are front and center, literally, as they are shown off with an ever changing rotation of tight shirts and revealing blouses tucked into tight skirts.

Trudy often waves to me with an enthusiastic "glad to see you" kind of wave. Everything about Trudy is big and boisterous. She epitomizes all that my mother tells me is against the rules for women to follow. To me, Trudy is unfathomable and I am utterly fascinated with her despite my mother's constant warnings to steer clear of such "unbecoming behavior", as she calls it.

Walking past Trudy, I wonder how many times she's had sex. I presume a lot. I often think to myself, "God, I hope I don't die before I get to do it." Though I know that happy day is far, far away as I am bound by the nice Jewish girl rules, which are clear and unalterable. The rules say, "I must be a virgin when I marry. I must marry a nice Jewish boy with prospects, hopefully from a rich family. This marriage must happen by the time I graduate from college." Until then I must repeat the word "No", as in "No, you can't touch me there, I am a nice Jewish girl!" The rules, however, are totally unclear on how do I keep "the nice Jewish boy" interested in me all the while I'm proclaiming "No!"

*For all those who were living out sexual fantasies society considered taboo, there were tens of millions of more women and men who were suppressing their sexuality and living a life of quiet desperation.*

If you are beautiful it must be easier to keep a guy's interest in you, even if you are a prude. But, I am only cute. How will I handle that? I have no clue. I didn't have a big sister or older friends whom I could go to for clarification. There was just my mom and she wasn't about to indulge my

268

questions about sex with an answer that made any sense in the real world.

Since I started elementary school, I've known that men have penises and I know they use them for peeing. The mystery at that point in my young life was – what do they use for sex? You may laugh and think that is odd for a girl in the 7th grade to not know nowadays, but back then it was not at all uncommon for girls and boys my age to be completely ignorant of the realities of sex. This was a time long before the Internet and far removed from the age of transparency.

I remember thinking if men have another thing they use for sex, where is it located? When I actually learn that they pee and engage in sex with the same thing, I am horror struck. How do they not make a mistake and pee inside you? Despite the myriad of questions and curiosities about sex that whirl in my head, I can see that Trudy looks happy all the time. I surmised it must be from all the sex she is having. "Oh my, what must that be like?" I wondered.

Like so many of my age during that era we sought out alternative means to satisfy our curiosity. One such occasion, I remember being in my 7th grade gym class, sitting in our white shorts on the bleachers, huddled together passing around a dog-eared copy of *Peyton Place*. We girls giggled and made funny faces to cover our embarrassment over reading the sex passages. Wide-eyed, I remember one classmate exclaiming, "I'll never do that." In a hushed tone I said, "Wow, so that's how it's done!"

Of course I had no idea how much sex Trudy was having, but that didn't stop my curious mind from creating all sorts of fanciful scenarios. As I would pass by her I wondered if my stares gave away the wild, passionate imaginings I had of her life inside that trailer. Also, I couldn't understand how Trudy was not ashamed of her behavior. The world I am raised in frowns on such overt displays of confidence in a woman. How could she get away with her daring outfits and scandalous lifestyle? I even wondered if she had a Prince Charming or if he'd left out of embarrassment.

To my mother and the rules of women for that period of time, Trudy represented the loose, low class woman who unapologetically flaunted her sexuality and drank too much. Perhaps that was true, but the dawn of a new age of sexual exploration was about to explode. The infamous Summer of Love was just around the corner for my generation and none of us had a clue what this meant or how much our ideas about sex, let alone ourselves, would change our lives and the world we lived in.

## THE SEXUAL REVOLUTION

My generation may have grown up naïve about sex, but by the time we were in college and entering the world of adulthood, a full-blown sexual revolution was underway, or was it? The so-called Summer of Love came

*Contrary to the wild stories that some recount, for most of us it was not a gregarious act of 24/7 sexual conquests.*

without warning but, looking back, the signs and patterns were clear. Just as it was with all topics associated with the rising tide of tension between Boomers and our parent's generation, we were tired of being kept in the dark, our youthful exuberance repressed in a tightly controlled set of rules that were not relevant to us. And what better way to explore adulthood and that of our own sense of self-worth than through sex?

As I got older, I can tell you there were many women of my mother's generation, and that of my own generation, who outwardly appeared to follow the strict rules of society,

271

warning against the act of sex or at least downplaying its role in our lives. Behind closed doors, however, it was an entirely different story as many of these same women were doing anything but living up to the lofty ideals they so quickly tore into others for not having. And then you had women and men who portrayed a sexy and loose image publicly, but behind closed doors their sex lives were non-existent. Some went as far as to tell false stories of sexual exploits, all in an attempt to fit in and feel acknowledged, despite how unflattering they made themselves look. Whether our generation, as a whole, was having lots of sex or not, there is a story that has not been told about the realities of the sexual revolution.

It is true, Baby Boomers ushered in the era of free love and the swinging 70's. What is not so openly talked about in all the articles, statistics and tongue-n-cheek stories about that time period is that it didn't occur for most of our generation. For all those who were living out sexual fantasies society considered taboo, there were tens of millions of more women and men who were suppressing their sexuality and living a life of quiet desperation. This would seem to contradict the free-spirited, rebellious descriptions often given to the sex, drugs and rock-n-roll era, which sells magazines, music and gets television ratings. While the stories and images are fun to hear and look at, they paint a picture of our lives that is anything but the way it was for most of us.

Like all the myths surrounding the Baby Boomer generation, the realities and lingering legacy of the sexual revolution are still being processed, particularly by those of us who lived through it. Contrary to the wild stories that some recount, for most of us it was not a gregarious act of 24/7 sexual conquests. For some, that may have been the case. But for the majority of Boomers entering the 70's as adults, there was the more pressing matter of survival. Trying to fit into society in ways that never seemed to live up to what we were told our lives were supposed to be like, was a harsh reality check. This included our experiences with sex, many of which were far less fulfilling than we had imagined.

Although we were exploring our sexuality in ways that flew in the face of the rigid ideas handed down to us from our parents, we were still naïve about the true nature of sex and how important it is to our mind, body and soul. We were no longer virgins, but all the sex in the world wasn't going to alter the reality of our lives. For most of us the fantasy of living happily ever after never happened. Or if it did, it was a less than easy road to happiness than we were told it would

273

be if we followed the rules and myths. The difficulties of navigating our adulthood meant abandoning the fantasies we had of freedom and self-expression. This opened the door to addictive behaviors to handle the mental, emotional and physical adjustments that few of us had been adequately prepared for.

Like so many women of my generation, I didn't marry a wealthy man. I had to hit the bricks so to speak not long after college. My husband and I had little time to do much else but create our own economic future. That point in life where I could hardly wait to experience sex had been replaced by the need to make a living. And sex wasn't paying the bills.

In ways that I can look back on and laugh, I essentially became Trudy. Of course I did not flaunt myself sexually in the way she did, but I was forced to use my talents to survive. In my case, my talents were creating and growing a business. Similar to Trudy, I rebelliously stepped out of the box women of my era were taught to stay in. Before the boom in women's entrepreneurism, which wouldn't come about for nearly 20 more years, there were not a lot of women in charge of companies in the 1970's. But here I was running a successful company with my husband.

During these business-building days, I had less time for sex than I would have ever thought I would when I was younger. It took me many years to realize just how important sex is to our mind, body and soul. While married, I joked that my husband and I were talking heads because our body's main purpose was to carry our heads around. So it was during this time in my life my mind was being used for business, my body as a means to carry around my head, and as for my soul, I never stopped to contemplate the power or role it had on living a joyous life. Something had to give and eventually my marriage and business came to an end. Little did I realize at the time, but this marked the re-birth of myself and ushered in my renaissance years.

## THE JOY OF LIVING

My mother lived for 25 years after my father's death. She joined a widow's group and built her new social life around the companionship with these other recently widowed women. I wanted her to meet and include new men into her life, but she refused. At no point did she ever discuss any affection for another man. Eventually, I realized her life was not mine. I loved my mother too much to try and circumvent her will.

While my situation after my divorce was far different than what my mother faced after my father's passing, I was faced with a decision I'd never thought about. I could join a divorced women's group, which to my surprise was more commonplace than I would have thought. I could involve myself in the singles scene, which I instinctively knew was not for me. Another option was to look inward and honor my desire to become an actor, essentially starting an entirely new life at a time when many my age were retiring. Although I was beginning to explore my sexuality on a level I'd repressed for many years, I was not about to leap out of my own skin and become someone I was not.

> *If we are changing how we view aging, than we must also change how we view our own sexuality as we age.*

One thing that is clear to me now, more than ever, is that we cannot escape the era we grew up in, which was rife with rebellious activities, specifically our involvement in sex. But, we also cannot afford to overlook how our upbringing about sex influenced us in ways that we are still grappling with. I do not believe our sexual appetite or how we view ourselves sexually should have to disappear, even if the person we were once intimate with does. My mother, like

276

many of her generation, enjoyed a vibrant and active life after the passing of her husband. So much of her own upbringing prepared her to turn off a switch internally and ignore a simple truth about herself. No matter how much we attempt to convince ourselves otherwise, we are sexual beings. Sex rounds out your *joie de vivre,* which is our joy of living.

Our physical health plays a significant role in our sexuality. There will come a point, though, where physical activities, such as sex, are not realistic due to health issues beyond the fix of a pill. Outside the obvious limitations brought on by severe health or physical ailments, we should not overlook the beauty and importance sexual arousal plays in maintaining the vibrancy of our own health. Even if we cannot engage in physical sex, we still have loving touches, holding hands, kissing and many other ways of expressing ourselves sexually that can expand and sustain a couple's love life.

## MY RENAISSANCE YEARS

More than any generation before us, Baby Boomers are defying the disengagement theory that for so long distorted our idea about what it means to live a long and fruitful life.

But if we are changing how we view aging, than we must also change how we view our own sexuality as we age.

This brings us back to a reoccurring theme of the book, which is to be grateful for where we are in life right now, not where we once were or where society says we should be. My 50's were my renaissance years. While I was feeling sexier at this stage of my life than ever before, and outpacing women half my age, I was not trying to be someone I wasn't. As much as we try to fit in and be seen, heard and loved, we should not lose sight of what is age appropriate. As the wonderfully gifted Joan Rivers once said, "Looking fifty is great, if you're sixty."

It is expected that we want to look our best and feel sexy, even if that means making some cosmetic upgrades or dressing in a way that is current with fashion trends. But if we are not comfortable in our bodies and accepting of who we are sexually, we can easily find ourselves doing things that are harmful to us physically, emotionally and mentally.

Not long after my divorce, I was wonderfully reconnected with a beautiful man I had met nearly 26 years earlier. Out of the blue he called me and I learned he had recently been through a divorce himself. Truth is, I was not thinking of involving myself with another man because my focus at the time was on me and my new career as an actress. Our friendship quickly gave way to a romance that blossomed because we were not closed off to a relationship, even though neither of us was actively pursuing one. His call and our subsequent dates reminded me of the power of being true to ourselves and not trying to control an outcome that is outside our control. By remaining non-attached to how things were unfolding romantically I learned a valuable lesson about being open to new experiences when life presents us a beautiful gift.

# Chapter 18

## ~ THE COFFEE DATE ~

*"What life means to us is determined not so much by what life brings us as by the attitude we bring to life; not so much by what happens to us as by our reaction to what happens."*

*Lewis Dunning*

I park the car, turn off the engine and immediately check my image in the rearview mirror. First I frown, as I definitely looked better in my bathroom mirror. Then I laugh at myself, remembering my mother's words "see how nice this is." She always said this when I didn't think the impending situation was going to turn out well, like doctor visits involving needles or eating strange foods. This time those words, "see how nice this is," refers to an arranged time to meet and greet a stranger at a public coffee house.

I am meeting a director for a future project. Outside of a couple of emails and a brief phone conversation, this is our first in-person encounter. Although this meeting carries no romantic overtones, there is a lot at stake here. As I am preparing to exit the car I am reminded that while a coffee date sounds simple, it isn't. The experience of connecting with someone new for the first time can be unnerving. Add in the elements of romance and it can be downright overwhelming.

Meant to be casual and inexpensive, what could be so hard about a coffee date? Plenty. Underneath this seemingly innocuous exchange between two people is an experience that is usually fraught with anxiety and unrealistic

*Rules for dating and the myths for living a fulfilling life varied from one family and culture to the next, but they all had one thing in common. Fear of love.*

expectations. Most people would not refer to a business meeting as a coffee date, but whether there is a chance for romance or not, these in-person get-togethers represent what is usually our first opportunity to further a connection that has likely taken place up to this point via email or phone.

A coffee date always carries three agendas. There's the agenda of the person we're meeting with, our own agenda and then the actual outcome that is going to happen, regardless of what either of us expect. More times than not, our agenda is laced with unrealistic concerns about what will unfold, be it good or bad. Most of these concerns are based on a flurry of contradictory thoughts about ourselves and unrealistic assumptions about romance. The worries we carry into these meetings take us out of the present moment as we focus more on what might happen than what is occurring in the now. This is especially true when the potentiality of romance is the primary reason for the initial coffee date.

A good portion of this book has been focused on breaking the myths we were raised on, and in doing so, removing the barriers to loving ourselves and living our best lives. Rarely did the seven myths work out for us as advertised. Thus, the rules and myths about sex and dating when we were younger are even more outdated now than they were when we actually believed they worked in our favor. But what if we still think and act as if dating and sexual activity in today's world is the same as the world we left a long time ago? It seems preposterous to believe that is the case. As we have seen in other areas of our lives, there is a code of conduct we were taught that still permeates our thoughts and behaviors today. Until we can open ourselves to a new way of seeing ourselves, and experiencing life through a revitalized lens, we will keep falling prey to a set of rules and myths that cannot be trusted as a reliable guide to navigate our romantic journey at this stage of our life.

## BEING AUTHENTIC

For most women and men of our generation, when we were young we believed we would find true happiness by adhering to the myths and rules handed down to us. The ever-present fear that our lives would be upended if we completely changed the status quo ensured most of us did not go too far in bending them, even if we were rebellious. Little did we know but the status quo was not designed from the heart. Rules for dating and the myths for living a fulfilling life varied from one family and culture to the next, but they all had one thing in common – fear of love. We were taught that love would hurt if we didn't obey the rules and myths. But, in following them we ended up getting hurt, and thus most of us convinced ourselves love was dangerous and could not be trusted.

We may have been passed over in favor of someone else early in life or we never seemed to live up to the high standards our parents and society set. Whatever it is that caused each of us to feel less than worthy, it most clearly showed up in our beliefs and experiences with dating, be it for romance, sex or both. After spending a lifetime believing we're not young enough, pretty enough or rich enough to attract and have love in our lives, it's time to turn the tables on what has prevented us from experiencing life to the fullest.

Self-love and seeing ourselves as our own Prince Charming is not about being an early bloomer or a late bloomer. We are perennial bloomers. And if we're going to enjoy the romance we deserve, it will require a lot more than just rehashing old paradigms. It's about being authentic and living not through someone else's perception of who they think we should be, but living the life deserving of who we really are. A key piece to manifesting such a change is approaching life experiences with a new set of questions, which are predicated on a new set of beliefs. For instance, how many of us women have gone on first dates saying to ourselves things such as, "He sounds so wonderful. Is he the one?" Or for many men it could be, "Does she or myself look like our pictures on the dating site? Will we disappoint each other? Will this lead to sex?"

Other common conversations we have with ourselves before meeting someone for the first time includes, "I should have lost the weight I was meaning to drop." "How will I handle the situation if we don't like each other?" Or worst still, "What if I like him and he doesn't like me? How humiliating if he asks for my phone number, I give it to him and then he never calls me." Shades of junior high and high school all over again!

These and many other similar questions race through our mind leading up to initial dates, each of them keeping us from being present and from being our genuine, authentic selves. Instead of putting so much pressure on ourselves, let us approach the meeting like it is a scene in a play or movie.

During the course of preparing to write this book, one thing I kept coming back to was how many of the skills I've acquired in acting can easily be applied to meeting new people for the first time. It turns out the skills needed for being a successful actor are remarkably similar for what is necessary for making dating more enjoyable and successful. As a simple way to rewrite the story of how and why we are meeting people for romantic purposes, I began constructing five transferable skills from acting to help people navigate this all-important first coffee date. Before we get into those skills there are some important elements that surround the idea of dating for Boomers that we should look at first.

## FULL CIRCLE

Our lives today are shaped by our experiences over the last 30 to 50 plus years. That's a lot of experiences and a lot of responsibilities that have accumulated over time. We know what we like and even if many of us are still searching for that elusive romantic partner, we have to realize we simply do not have the time to meet people like we once did. And when we do meet them for the first time, there's a lot we're bringing to the coffee date that we never imagined when we were in the dating scene in our 20's.

For Baby Boomers who find themselves single, there are many options in today's world for locating a mate that are totally new and quite foreign from how things were done "in the old days". The Internet has completely revolutionized how people

> *"50 marks the beginning of the best years of our lives, including the best sex of our lives."*
>
> Dr. Christiane Northrup

meet and connect. Technology and online dating has made it easier to narrow down a search to meet someone who is in alignment with where we are in life. No matter how savvy we may be with online dating profiles, or how adept we are at idle chitchat, dating in today's world for people of our generation can be scary. While I haven't been privy to all of the nuances and challenges of dating as many of my fellow Boomers have, I have spent a great amount of time speaking with and researching the various ups and downs that come with dating for my generation.

Of the nearly 80 million Baby Boomers in America, multiple studies indicate that over a third are single. Whether it is from divorce, being widowed or having never married, the surge in the dating scene is not surprisingly driven by Boomers. The leading online dating sites all report that the 55 and over demographic is the fastest growing. Surveys of online daters reinforce what so many of my own friends say, namely that both physical attraction and sexual intimacy are crucial for any short-term or long-term dating consideration.

We have come full circle. We have gone from an almost uncontrollable desire to let loose and explore sex in our physical youth, to not having time or energy for it during our prime money making years and now reclaiming the sexual nature of who we are. Rather than downplay our desires for sex, Boomers are now cultivating it in ways that are totally new to us.

Dr. Christiane Northrup, author of multiple best-selling books writes, "50 marks the beginning of the best years of our lives, including the best sex of our lives." With a new and refined way of seeing ourselves in the mirror and accepting sex does not die when we step into the 55 and over club, more than ever Boomers are revving up their sexuality. Chemistry has to be there in our connections and many speak of the importance of attraction that goes beyond just the physical. This is where the need for self-love is so important and with that acceptance comes the release of our need to set up scenarios that are ripe for disappointment.

## THE OVERWHELMING REALITY OF DATING

Despite the unmistakable change in how society communicates and connects through the world of technology, the same instinctual fears and desires of sex and dating are really no different today than they were three to four decades ago. We create scenarios that provide us opportunities to meet people, following our internal compass as to which of these people we want to spend more quality and intimate time with. The issue for Baby Boomers is that we've already done this.

Women and men over the age of 55 have to confront unique scenarios few other generations ever had to when it comes to dating. There are marriages and divorces, often more than one, plus children and grandchildren. The reality of moving on after spouses have died is something millions in our generation have had to contend with and still do. It is no secret that seven out of 10 Baby Boomer women will outlive their husbands, according to the U.S. Department of Health and Human Services. There is an inescapable reality for women that our present and future mates may get ill and we will be the ones saddled with the burden of caring for them. For anyone who has had to face the passing of a beloved, the idea of doing that all over again is beyond comprehension. None of this is to insinuate men of our generation do not face similar or the same inherent issues and challenges, because they do. The prospect of being unable to physically or financially take care of one's self in the not so distant future places Baby Boomers in some very unique situations when it comes to dating, particularly how to approach those initial coffee dates and setting realistic expectations.

With that in mind, let's take a moment to explore the five transferrable skills I've learned from the world of acting and how they directly apply to dating for Baby Boomers, specifically as it relates to enjoying the ubiquitous coffee date.

*SKILL #1 – KNOW WHO YOU ARE*

For an actor who is preparing for a role this skill is rarely overlooked, but in my experience it's not so obvious to people who are seeking someone to have a mutually fulfilling relationship with. The more self-aware we are, the less likely we will get involved with someone who is not well suited to our personality or lifestyle. If you are single and looking to find someone to spend your time with, it's important the change you seek in your life comes from within. An attempt to get what you want while secretly rejecting yourself will only lead to more unnecessary heartache, both for you and someone you want to have a relationship with.

Giving ourselves permission to love and be loved allows us to know what is really important in our lives. The key to knowing we are worthy of giving and receiving love is that it places us in the best possible position to not waste our time seeking people to be around us who are not in our best interest. Give some thought as to what traits are important in a person you want to date at this point in your life. Do these traits align with your own? And how do they synch up with the lifestyle you see yourself living today? Are you being the person you seek, as much as being the change you seek?

You cannot look for someone to fulfill your deficits, which is to say you cannot expect someone to provide you what you are lacking within. People are

> *Attracting the ideal person in our lives comes down to learning to first love ourselves.*

always saying how much happier they would be if someone was in their life. But who wants to be with someone who is miserable? A person who is unhappy will likely be uncomfortable receiving love because they have yet to look within themselves and accept the fact that they are truly worthy of self-love. You have to own what it is you are looking for by being what it is you seek.

Attracting the ideal person in our lives comes down to learning to first love ourselves. To love who we are is less about being narcissistic and more about knowing we are worthy of giving and receiving love. We must never forget we are our own Prince Charming.

I'm not suggesting that every first date you go on is about finding the love of your life. As an actor not every audition I go on is going to land me an Oscar opportunity. With each audition and new role I play, I am giving myself permission to let go of fears and step into the unknown. It is here that I will tap into the true essence of whatever character I'm playing. The same holds true for unleashing the real you in any situation you're called into, particularly for a coffee date.

## SKILL #2 – KNOW WHAT YOU WANT TO ACCOMPLISH

Of all the things an actor has to do to prepare for a scene, nothing is as important as knowing what you want to accomplish. This applies just as equally to dating. If you do not know what you want to achieve by the end of your coffee date, you will end up confusing activity with accomplishment, resulting in an outcome that is less than desired.

Let's take a casual coffee date and compare that to a mini-scene with another actor. In this scenario you will want to arrive on set (at the date) with an energy that isn't to control the interaction, but to give the other person your full attention. What is it that you want? What are you listening for? What resonates with you emotionally? What causes you to laugh?

Every date is important, even the ones that seem to be little more than a meet and greet. Just like every scene or audition an actor is in, there is always something at stake. Some people, like actors, relegate dates and scenes to the mundane and give little importance to them. Actors who do this are rarely successful, just as people who do this will likely not have enjoyable dates or meaningful relationships.

There's a fine line between making the moment more than what it is and dismissing the person you're engaging with by giving little importance to your scene or date with them. So be sure to raise the stakes and realize that every scene and every date, no matter how big or small it may appear to be, is important because you're in it. Don't overlook that it's important for the other person you're interacting with. They have an agenda just as you do, which is usually to arrive at an enjoyable outcome no different than you.

When it comes to coffee dates, though, someone else's idea of accomplishing a desired outcome could be very different than your own. Know what you want to accomplish, but surrender the attachment to expectations so that you can actually be present in the moment. This allows you to not get caught up in a fantasy that is not mutually beneficial for you and the person you're connecting with.

## *SKILL #3 – KNOW WHAT MOTIVATES YOU TO SPEAK*

Every good actor knows the importance of being aware of what motivates a character to speak as they do. Just as an actor gets into the mindset of the character they are playing, it is equally important for you to be aware of the mindset and motivation necessary for you to talk during a coffee date.

This can be applied to any area of life. Just as an actor may not have any upcoming roles or auditions they are aware of, that doesn't stop them from preparing. If you don't see yourself going on a coffee date anytime soon, consider what motivates you to speak in the situations you do find yourself in.

> *Listening is at the top of the list for making a coffee date an enjoyable experience, just as it is for ensuring a successful scene for an actor.*

It is one thing to know why you are speaking, but do you know what you are listening for? In life, good listeners are rare and always highly valued. Listening is at the top of the list for making a coffee date an enjoyable experience, just as it is for ensuring a successful scene for an actor. To have a better understanding of how important listening is for an actor, consider how the camera loves the reaction shot in both TV and movie scenes. The camera shows the listener and his reaction to what is being said, not the speaker of the words. Actors, therefore, are listening more than just performing.

Every television show, film and play speaks a language all its own. The same can be said for every coffee date. There is a unique exchange that unfolds when two people meet. Whether those two connect on a romantic level or not, there is a language being spoken and the one who listens with a genuine intent to hear what is being said is the one who remains present and never gets lost in what they are experiencing.

When it comes to what motivates you to speak or getting your partner to talk, perhaps nothing can turn the tide of an audition or a date like asking the question, *"Tell me about yourself?"* Those in charge of the audition want to know an actors' story and the same can be true for someone who asks you this question on a date. This is not an open invitation to talk about why you wanted to be an actor, or to talk about all of your past relationships, medical issues or life regrets. These topics are important, but they're not the best for immediately engaging someone.

No one wants to hear your entire life story, so it's important to know yourself well enough to be comfortable talking about your life in a way that is engaging and intriguing. Learn to tell a good story, which will always involve some level of conflict in it. Whether it's recognizing and resolving conflict, it is a driving factor in stories.

All good stories contain the following elements: surprise, funny one-liners, urgency/time limits and suspense. Your listener will be captivated and eager to hear your unfolding story. Be mindful that the outcome of your story is not revealed until the story's ending. Create stories that really show off your personality and let your light shine. Thus, your next coffee date will be framed with a wonderful story of yourself.

## SKILL #4 – KNOW WHAT YOU WANT FROM OTHERS IN A SCENE

Actors are notorious for asking "What is my character's motivation?" Rarely, however, do actors wonder about the motivation of the other characters in the scene. This oversight is equally crucial for anyone going on a coffee date. Our motivation for what we want out of a date at this point in our lives can be vastly different from what motivated us to go on dates earlier in our life.

Earlier in life our dates were framed by how society expected us to live. Find a suitable mate, get married, have a family, earn a living and live happily ever after. What about now? What motivates Boomers to get out of our daily routine and meet someone whom we know little to nothing about? Whatever our motivation is for going on a date, there is something motivating the person who will be sitting across from us. It's our job to understand what that is and determine if it is in alignment with ours.

> *Our motivation for what we want out of a date at this point in our lives can be vastly different from what motivated us to go on dates earlier in our life.*

When we don't take time to understand the desired outcome or agenda of the other person, the outcome is no different than when an actor enters a scene arrogantly, assuming they already know what the other actor is going to do. What results is usually a disaster. Surrendering the need to assume an expected outcome requires us to be present and in tune with the person we're meeting with, as much as it is necessary to be in tune with what we want out of this encounter.

Actors have to have a relationship with everything they interact with in a scene. This ranges from a prop to other actors and the environment the scene is supposed to be taking place in. If we're not in tune with all of this, the acting will come off as contrived and the entire scene is thrown out of balance. This is why knowing what you want from others in a scene is a transferable skill from acting to dating. If you are on a date and not focused on the person you're meeting or out of tune with the environment the date is taking place, the entire experience will be thrown out of whack.

While all of this may seem really obvious, the reality is that most people take very little time to know themselves, let alone be fully aware of what it is they really want from a coffee date. Some think all that is necessary is to dress up and show up. This can be a challenge for Baby Boomers as many of us have gone a decade or more without being on a date. As a result, it is not uncommon for people in those situations to arrive on a coffee date with superficial intentions and unrealistic motivations that are out of sync with the person they are meeting with.

So the next time you find yourself on a coffee date, approach your desired outcome like a highly trained actor authentically approaches a scene. Know what you want out of the experience, but be prepared to let go of this desire so as to be in tune with the person you're exchanging time with. Doing so will go a long way to positively creating a mutually beneficial outcome for everyone.

## SKILL #5 – KNOW WHAT IS AT STAKE FOR YOU

Actors have a commitment to what they are saying and doing. A good actor will not only know what is at stake for their character in one scene, but is keenly aware of how the scene affects the character in all other scenes *(i.e. the emotional arc of the character)*. In much the same way, knowing what is at stake for you on a coffee date goes beyond just the date itself. Every experience we have has a ripple effect for other areas of our life. Nowhere is this more relevant than it is for Baby Boomers who are dating.

By the time we've reached the age of 55 or older, we have spent a lifetime preparing for this stage of our life. It is not surprising to discover it is nothing like we thought it would be. What is at stake in dating someone, be it casual or a serious relationship, can and often does carry far greater consequences than at any other point in our life because of what we have been through and what we are no longer willing to tolerate. So you can see why it's important to be aware of what is at stake, even if it is just a coffee date.

This is why staying present allows us not to get carried away with unrealistic expectations or get caught up with our own story or that of another. We've all been in situations where we lose sense of the moment and end up falling in love with our own voice. Many times people will talk incessantly on coffee dates, but the opposite holds true as well. If someone you meet is shy and defers to you to carry the conversation, you will want to be prepared to carry the conversation. This may not be an easy thing to do if you yourself are shy.

When in doubt about what is at stake, or what to say, always remember to love who you are, be with those you enjoy and do what you love. When we accept we are our own Prince Charming it becomes impossible not to genuinely be at ease no matter what the outcome of any coffee date or situation we find ourselves in. In that state of mind we will never settle for less than what we deserve.

# Chapter 19

## ~ ALL IS WELL ~

*"The closer you get to the summit the harder the climb."*
*Joanie Marx*

For one month straight I spent every day with my beloved mother in the hospital. Like much of our relationship through the years, that long, arduous stay in the hospital was a journey of hope and despair wonderfully blended in with real, genuine moments of beautifully connecting with one another from our heart and soul. Of course, the length and scope of our conversations were severely limited due to her brief moments of lucidity. Even so, the deep gratitude and mutual admiration we had built up over the years was unmistakably present in those precious moments of my mother's coherency.

This last month in the hospital all started with a simple infection that worsened and ended with renal failure. For the first half of the month my mother was in that grey space between getting better and getting worse. While she struggled to get better I brought family pictures and a shoe box of letters that we had written to one another during those times we were not near each other. I would sit by her side and wait for these precious moments of fleeting alertness which I filled by reading these heartfelt letters and showing her the pictures. When she smiled with recognition, the room filled with light and for that glorious moment everything was fine. Hope was restored. But this would not last.

I remember vividly the moment during her final month when all hope was gone and the reality of her condition and what it meant for her life, and my own, came

> *By the end of the month my mother's body did not have the capacity to live anymore. Perhaps hardest of all, was seeing this and realizing she wasn't dead either.*

crashing down on me. It was around the half-way point of her stay in the hospital. I was in my mother's room when her doctor came in to discuss the most recent x-ray results. He started the conversation by asking my mother routine questions that she should have been able to answer, even though her sense of awareness would ebb and flow. On this day, the questions were not registering at all and she had no answer for any of them. There was a brief pause between questions and then the doctor asked my mother the most basic of all, "What is your name?"

303

My mother thought for a moment while I quietly held my breath. She looked up at him and said, "Well, you know how that is." She let out a hearty laugh in a failed attempt to cover up what was painfully obvious. She did not know her own name.

I found myself feeling a sense of hopelessness I never knew existed. Here is the strongest woman I've ever known, someone I had looked to for guidance and support all my life, and she has been reduced to uttering a thinly veiled attempt to hide the unmistakable truth; she doesn't know who she is. I felt like a little 5 year old who has to reconcile the impossible reality that her mother is gone. Sure, she was there physically, but once this threshold of not knowing who you are had been crossed, coupled with the reality of her condition, there was no turning back. I just wanted to crumble and cry, but I couldn't.

The doctor and I exchanged glances, both of us understanding what this latest turn of events represented for my mother. Unlike the doctor's more detached demeanor, for me this situation was heartbreaking beyond anything I could describe then, or even now.

## NOT AN EASY THING TO RECONCILE

By the end of the month my mother's body did not have the capacity to live anymore. Perhaps hardest of all, was seeing this and realizing she wasn't dead either. I had directed the medical staff to do everything within the realm of possibility to facilitate her getting better. To their credit they had done so. And now, after a tense consultation with her doctors, I have been tasked with making a fateful decision to end her life or allow what was left of it to continue on.

As I sat beside her, fully aware that the hardest decision of my life needed to be made right away, it became apparent what must be done. I leaned over my mother and gently whispered in her ear, "I see that you want to live, so we will do desperate measures -- whatever it takes to help you." Willing herself back from the depth of her deathbed, my mother slowly opened her eyes and looked at me. I could see she was aware of the moment and it was one of those precious seconds of Mother Charming returning. I knew this was fleeting, but it also reinforced my decision that as long as she wanted to live, I would in no way authorize the doctors to end her life. I would not kill my mother.

305

She lifted her hand and I leaned in further so that she could stroke my cheek. For that instant, she was my mother caring for me; giving me love and strength. She could not speak, but her message was crystal clear, "All is well. Everything is fine just the way it is. I am fine and so are you. Nothing more needs to be done." Her love for me shone in her eyes and I could not help but be transported back to those enchanting moments when she would read to me when I was a young child. We had returned to "My Blue Heaven."

I held onto her hand, allowing it to remain against my skin for longer than she would have been able to hold it there. She was still coherent as I said to her, "I love you more than anyone in this world has ever loved you." This registered with my mother and then I could see the light go out and she drifted back into that silent void between life and death.

## I'LL BE RIGHT BACK

I notified the doctors of my decision that night. Two days later mother slipped into a coma, that inward focus, shutting down phase. She entered the final preparatory stage of dying. No more talking. No more temporary moments of clarity.

It took several more days for the end to officially arrive. Each of those days I remained at her side, holding her hand.

306

Sitting beside her, I remembered how I felt as a little girl when I couldn't talk because my throat hurt. My mother would patiently sit on the edge of my bed as I lay still with closed eyes, resting in the security of her comforting presence. During many years of my adulthood, accentuated by those moments of quiet despair and loneliness, I would have given anything to go back to those times where nothing in the world mattered but the love and security of my mother.

It's true there were stretches of my childhood and well into my adult life where my mother wasn't there for me as I would have liked. As easy as it would have been to hold her responsible for her lack of advice when I needed it or the absence of support when I yearned for it, I could not have overlooked how she prepared me to be the person I grew into. For it was in those moments of feeling all was lost, underlined by the inner strength my mother instilled in me, I came to meet my Prince Charming. How else could I have navigated this journey of my life if it had not been for my mother?

*How else could I have navigated this journey of my life if it had not been for my mother?*

Long before my mother reached this point I had forgiven her for whatever wrongs I had perceived she made. Those ideas of competing with her expectations of me and believing I could never measure up had evaporated with the past. She and I had gotten through so much together. It was during our golden years, when I was married and running the business with Allan, that mother and I clicked on all cylinders. During this glorious time our relationship had fulfilled its most beautiful potential.

The last morning of her life, I stopped off at the market and got three big balloons: one in pink, dark pink and the third being purple. My mother always loved balloons. I brought them to her bed and tied them to the bed rail as the nurse gave my mother a sponge bath. I brushed her hair and after the nurse changed her gown, I leaned over and gave her a kiss on the forehead, and said, "I'll be right back."

Moments after I left the room my mother passed away. Maybe she was waiting for that moment to go. She always said, "You come into this world alone and you go out the same way." Returning to her room I saw that indeed she was gone. I re-tied the balloons to her wrist nametag. Her body was lifeless, but above her the floating balloons spoke of airiness and joy brightening the room with color, not darkness or sadness.

## THE LITTLE THINGS

I was not aware of it while she was alive, but I am now; not all Baby Boomers can claim to have had the kind of relationship my mother and I did. In breaking the myths associated with our generation, and by sharing my story, perhaps those who read this can find it within their heart to forgive their parents and in return, forgive themselves.

Despite what each of us have been through over the years, it is with a deep sense of gratitude for the little things, bolstered by our forgiveness, that can and will light the path we travel. It's very easy to highlight the big achievements of our lives and say that's what we're grateful for. In doing so, we overlook the little things that are the pillars that hold up our lives, providing us the space and time to achieve the bigger accomplishments.

Those final days with my mother were not so much a time of sorrow as it was a time of appreciating the love that had been shared. It was the little things we had experienced together that illuminated what could have been the darkest days of my life. These were the thoughts that had sustained

309

me for so long and I was not about to abandon them in favor of grief.

In the days leading up to her passing I opened myself up to acknowledge and embrace the little things that we so often take for granted in our fast-paced life. I took in and gave thanks for the ray

*Through all of this I realize now that my mother is that bright star which forever brightens my path, then and now.*

of sun that fell across my mother's face with wonderful warmth. I breathed in the sweet aroma of life that filled her hospital room from the freshly cut flowers on the table. I even found myself looking forward to hearing the little tune the kind nurse sang when she bathed my mother each day. And I found myself returning to the phrase, "born under a lucky star", which has so often been an anchor in my life. Through all of this I realize now that my mother is that bright star which forever brightens my path, then and now.

## COVERING THE DISTANCE

As I prepared my eulogy, I rummage through boxes of old letters. Several of them I had compiled into one box, which I took with me to the hospital during my mother's stay. I come across one I had overlooked previously. It was a letter my mother had written to me after I had moved to Berkeley to attend the University. She talks briefly about how she and my father handled "the loss of their little girl" that no longer lived at home. How daddy kept setting the table for three, looking to the driveway at 5:35 pm expecting me to drive in, and how the house is now too clean and quiet.

In September, they came up for Parent's Weekend and she writes to me about their experience. My father asks her to include his thoughts, which were, "Mother and I both had one grand weekend with you. You were sweet, interesting, just enough ladylike and yet just enough childlike. Thanks again for the swell weekend."

My mother wrote later in the letter that, "Daddy and I wanted to call you last night because we hadn't heard from you since we dropped you off on a strange corner in San Francisco. For some undefined reason this bothered me all week. It may account for the fact that this second parting was worse for me than the first, when we dropped you off at the airport to fly to Cal. Daddy mentions quite often that you may not like it at Cal after all and that you will want to continue your education at UCLA."

Later on in the letter she shared that, "Last night I told daddy to quit feeding himself the panacea and finally face once and for all the fact that you are GONE. I sat on the front porch one warm, dark night after returning from San Francisco and came to grips with myself and the situation. There is no comfort to be gained from such a confrontation, but it settles the mind."

Always careful not to be misunderstood, my mother clarified her remarks in the letter by adding, "Please do not misunderstand and think that we do not want you to be away from home. It is not that at all. We are happy that you realized your dream to attend the University and we feel it is the best thing in the world for you. It is difficult, however, to break 20 years of habit. I think the fact that we did not phone you last night proves that we are making headway. Probably individually and acting alone, each of us would have called, but together we stood firm."

Mind you, this was a time long before computers and cell phones. Distance did mean separation and long stretches of it. The only instant connection was by expensive long distance phone calls. Baby Boomers reading this will remember just how costly and brief those calls were. The space between my parents and I was filled by letters either typed or hand written. There was a lot of emotion, both overt and restrained, that filled the ink of those words.

## IN MY MOTHER'S OWN WORDS

Now, here I sat having to use words to summarize my mother's life in a way that was deeply personal and private. She was well admired by a great many in the community for the creative work she had done over the years. It was disconcerting that I would have to cover such a great distance of time to encapsulate who my mother was, not only to me and my daddy, but to all those who had crossed paths with her over the years.

My mother cast a very long shadow. She kept her own counsel, innately knew and followed the principle, "I came into this world to be myself, for that I came." Somehow it was easy for her. Always herself, with all the simplicity and complexity that was her, she loved my daddy and me and

313

treated the people she allowed into her inner circle with great respect. She had a quick mind, a keen sense of humor and a wonderful writing style. A woman of enormous creative talent, my mother displayed little drive to succeed in the traditional sense. She admired lovely things, but didn't feel a need to own them. Neither money nor status concerned her. Although a perfectionist, she had a very hard time accepting a compliment. In retrospect, this hindered her ability to see the splendid beauty in what she herself did.

My mother always said, "Her fifties and sixties were her best decades." This, of course, really didn't register with me until I crossed into those years myself and her words proved to be an inspiration for me at that time in my life. She had many artist friends and belonged to several leagues. Mother was immersed in her art, attended several weekly classes, did day paint-outs, exhibited her work in art shows, sold paintings and then always regretted selling each and every picture.

In a catch-up letter to her sister Sarah she wrote, "Sam has been retired now for over a year due to poor health and so we do all the things retired people do. Mainly look for free entertainment, visit old friends and shoot the breeze, take picnic lunches to the seaside and paint the scenery. Allow me to brag a bit. Watercolor West is a very prestigious transparent watercolor society; one of the three best on the national scene. It is considered an honor to be invited to show, never mind being 'juried in' to hang in the show. I've dragged Sam there for years to see the show. Well, to make a long but wonderful story short, my entry was hung in the show. It was a great ego trip, that euphoric feeling like being in love."

I got great joy out of reading this, for it is one of those rare occasions in my mother's life where she openly admitted a sense of happiness at being recognized and acknowledged for the wonderfully gifted artist that she was. I continued to go through these letters and came across a piece my mother had written about herself that was published for the Mid-Valley Art League monthly newsletter. My mother was asked to write about herself for the "Getting to Know You Column." I realized that while I could stay quite a bit about my mother, perhaps the eulogy would be best served to have my mother's own words speak for her.

## NO LONG SHADOWS

My mother started off the column with, "Betty, you have stuck me with the obligation of writing about myself for your column. Anyone else would have gotten a flat "no", but you know I cannot refuse your request. There isn't much to tell about myself, but here goes a capsule of a capsule.

My faculty of almost total recall of early childhood has mainly proved to be a disadvantage. In certain specific cases I can dig down and remember exactly what occurred at a given time.

*"It is the light that brightens my life and despite the pile-up of years, there are still no long shadows."*

The childhood anxieties, the sights, sounds, smells and thoughts that passed through my mind from a child's perspective remain clear. One of my earliest recollections is that of great preoccupation with light falling on an object and casting a shadow. Another wonderful mystery was the refraction of light in water and the colors cast by sunlight through colored glass. And prisms, oh, there was a miracle! This is still the way I view the world around me. What I really look at are the ever-changing patterns of light and shadows on simple objects which transfix them into design worthy to be painted.

Some years ago, I discovered watercolor and felt in my bones that I had found my medium at last. The elusive, wild, unpredictability of watercolor is a challenge which is never satisfied. Rarely has the idea I had in mind at the beginning of a painting ever reached my expectations. Perhaps over the years, four or five paintings have ever 'made it', which translates to a lot of wasted paper, used on both sides yet! When starting a painting, I concern myself first with the passage of light and dark running through the composition. Subject matter emerges as a second consideration."

In another part of the piece, she writes, "I find it difficult to paint what I see. There is an inner memory of childhood days in the Midwest prairie states which changes California palm trees to dark cottonwoods and yellow grass to snowdrifts. After having lived over thirty years in California, I still have not come to grips with desert landscape. Somewhere in my painting a bit of water seems to always appear, if only in a puddle or a wheel rut."

My mother concluded her column with, "Painting is important to me and the companionship of fellow artists in the classroom and at League meetings is a great joy to me. It is the light that brightens my life and despite the pile-up of years, there are still no long shadows.

When the article was printed in the Newsletter there had been a drastic change. Now there was a long shadow. My father had just died. He had been her life-long champion, the one whose light brightened up her days. From that day on my mother never again picked up a paintbrush. With her great love now gone, so too was her love for painting.

## TOGETHER AGAIN

The day before the funeral I carefully washed and ironed a lovely floral shirtwaist dress and yellow cardigan sweater that my mother will wear into eternity. My daddy always said, "It is always better to take a sweater with you. You might not need it, but if you do, you can't put on a sweater you don't have with you."

After I dropped off my mother's clothes at the funeral hall I grabbed something to eat at a nearby Chinese restaurant. After the meal I read my fortune cookie, which said something about the achievement of a goal being similar to climbing a mountain. The analogy stuck with me and when I arrived home I wrote down my own thoughts about this, which came out to be, "The closer you get to the summit the harder the climb." Not often does a fortune cookie inspire someone to reframe a life-altering experience, but on that day and in that moment I could not help but be profoundly grateful for my parents and all they did to help me achieve my goals and reach the summit of my life.

That same day I stopped by where my father's ashes had been placed many years before. He wanted to be cremated. Mother and I

*The closer you get to the summit the harder the climb.*

scattered his ashes on the ground just before our warehouse foundation was poured for the business I had started with Allan. Standing sentinel at the edge of the property is a tall tree called a Beef Wood Tree. Since my daddy was a meat and potato man, we all thought it was perfect. From my reckoning, my mother's desk at our business was over the ashes beneath the foundation. I always felt that we were all together during those years of the business and that daddy watched over us. Perhaps it was that unspoken knowledge that our family was together that helped bring out the spark in my mother and strengthened our bond. Whatever it was, those years with my mother were pure magic.

319

Standing there before the Beef Wood tree, I leaned down and scooped up a cup of dirt. I closed the lid to this cup and planned on placing it inside my mother's coffin the next day. My parents would be together again. All was well.

*IN MY HEART*

In Jewish tradition, the yearlong mourning period is officially ended by the unveiling of the headstone. As the time approached to come up with what to say on my mother's headstone, I received a timely and deeply loving poem about my mother from Elaine, my college roommate. Elaine, Sue and I have been best friends and sisters starting from the first day of our happenstance meeting at our UC Berkeley residency hall. We were total strangers, each with our few belongings, looking to make a home for ourselves. Instead of living together for a temporary time, we made a permanent place in each of our hearts for the three of us to live and flourish.

Upon reading what Elaine wrote, it was clear she had captured the purest essence of who my mother was. Etched into the stone commemorating my parents are my words about my father and Elaine's poem about my mother. They are as follows:

### *My Father – The Inspirer*

A poem of life and everything between the lines

Loved by his wife

Adored by his daughter

And liked by one and all

### *My Mother – The Artist*

My life was a painting

It was drawn that way

From vivacious vermilion to soft, subtle gray

And all the hues that blaze in the light

Dance with their shadows across my sight

I look with an eye concealed in my heart

Hoping to capture a piece of the art

That lies beyond what the eye can see

Transferring to canvas its vision for me

It crystallized there, forever true

Forever old, forever new

Memories fleeting, yet never to cease

Encased in color, of me...a piece

# Chapter 20

## ~ HERE IS PRETTY GOOD ~

*"Face the sun, the shadows will be behind you."*
*A New Zealand Maori Proverb*

The streets are familiar. Little has changed in 48 years. As I round the corner of my mother's neighborhood, I see the bright pink sign that says, "Estate Sale" with a big black vinyl arrow and a street address. My home address, the same one I have written on envelopes and post cards for my entire life. I know the signs will be up. I know the sale is on. I organized it. Still the vision of the street post with the sign catches me by surprise and for a moment, takes my breath away.

I see another pink estate sale sign poked into the front lawn. Cars line the street in front of my house. I don't recognize any of these cars. The people who own the cars are filing through the rooms of my mother's home looking for bargains. They are not family, nor are they friends. In fact, my mother had no friends in the years leading up to her death. Her dementia had caused all her life-long friends to flee, as if what she had was a disease that could be caught. Such is the myth of aging.

During the last several years of my mother's life the only people who came to her home were those I paid to be there. As a child she always told me that I didn't have any friends because I didn't know

*Time does march on. It waits for no one. Even the weariest river winds safely home to sea.*

how to be a genuine friend to anybody. The really sad part is that I believed she was right for a good portion of my life.

I walk up the driveway and enter a backyard dotted with card tables filled with household items. How strange that our family possessions are lying outside. Inside my mother's furniture is there just not in their right places. Absent are the wonderful cooking aromas from the bubbling pots on the kitchen stove. My past has been wiped away by the smell of 409 and Windex. Nothing about this feels like my home. As I walk through the rooms the loss is heavier and more real than I had led myself to believe.

Outside my favorite peach tree stands motionless, yet I feel this fierce force scattering my childhood home to the winds, where the reality of it will exist only in my dreams. I try to convince myself it is all right to feel the pain, mourn the loss and acknowledge the passage of time. It took a very long time to fully grow up, but now it is a done deed. There is no place to go and feel special. No place to go and tangibly see my childhood. The realization I have no childhood home to go to, no parents waiting at the door to see "the little girl" floods my mind with a cascading array of emotions. I have to get out of here. As I turn to leave the woman conducting the estate sale stops me. She asks if I want to look through the unsold items and take more things with me.

This interruption halts the emotional void I was being engulfed by, awakening me to an idea I'd known but never fully accepted. Time does march on. It waits for no one. Even the weariest river winds safely home to sea.

I take an inventory of my emotions. A rising tide of confidence is emerging where a moment earlier an overwhelming feeling of helplessness had taken hold. I take a deep breath, inhaling a lifetime of memories. I quietly and calmly exhale, letting go of my attachments to a past that is no longer in the here and now. My eyes scan the remains, each item calling out to me. Remember me. Take me. Don't abandon me. Love me.

I hold my hands up – enough! I can absorb and take no more of the past. I am entitled to my space for my own things. I will no longer lose myself and my own self-identity in things that no longer fit into the life that I am here to live in this moment. I must have boundaries. In this empty space that echoes in my heart, I will plant the seeds and cultivate a new life. I will survive and flourish.

I walked away from that estate-sale without taking one single item.

*STEPPING INTO YOUR HAPPINESS*

With our age come losses. No amount of fun, money or distinguished titles is going to change the reality that we all pass on from this world. I am reminded of this by my dear friend, Neil, who was the first close friend from my generation to die.

We met when he was 16 and I was 14 years old. As he said to me on our last phone call, "I am battling the monster growing inside of me that wants to kill me." The reality of what was happening to him, along with a jarring sense of fear and panic I could hear in his voice, froze me. It had been several years since mother died and I felt ill-equipped to provide a comforting reply to him. My philosophy about

325

death and what happens as we journey into eternity was further shaped by that conversation as much as my mother's passing.

After our call I felt compelled to write a letter to Neil. In my letter I conveyed my heartfelt thoughts. As we all contemplate the unknown, my point of view on how to handle it is to decide which moment in this life has made you the happiest. Fix that image in your mind. Then when the unknown time comes, you step into your happiness. If the last thought you have is your happiest moment, it is this moment that becomes the last experience of your life. Can we not make this the happiest moment of all? Who is to say whether you will experience it for eternity? Even if it does not continue into eternity, if it only exists as the last conscience thought that you have in your body, than that is enough.

> *"I am grateful for the gifts of intelligence, love, wonder and laughter. You can't say it wasn't interesting."*
>
> *Roger Ebert*

Neil died a week after I sent him the letter. I will never know if he actually was able to read it. I'd like to think he did. Unable to attend the actual funeral, the following week I make it a point to drive to the cemetery where Neil is buried to say goodbye. On a knoll with a lovely view I found his plot. There is a small, green edged, clear plastic flat marker patted into the matted grass bearing his name and funeral date. Nothing more.

There is something on this day that strikes a chord with me that I had not fully comprehended before. I take in the surroundings and nowhere to be found are anyone's earthly possessions. There are no U-Hauls that follow the numerous hearses that come in and out of this cemetery. No calendar of upcoming events are listed on the tombstones. There is no sign of lengthy "to-do" lists filled with self-imposed deadlines, endless worries and dreams of future accomplishments. Perhaps most telling, there are no signs or lists of regrets, grievances and or "do-overs". There's not even a Wi-Fi signal here.

I bear witness to the arc of Neil's life from a boy to our last conversation, when he didn't know what to make of his own impending death. One of the last things I remember him saying was, "I don't know, I just don't know."

327

I bend down and place a small rock on his plot. In the Jewish tradition, a placed rock signifies that someone is watching over this grave. A stone costs no money. It is the gesture and symbol of the watchful eye that is important. Standing up, my eyes remain fixed on the stone. Here I am reminded of a quote from Roger Ebert, the famous movie critic, who said he did not fear death because he didn't believe there was anything "on the other side of death to fear. I was perfectly content before I was born, and I think of death as the same state," he wrote. "I am grateful for the gifts of intelligence, love, wonder and laughter. You can't say it wasn't interesting."

As I walk to my car, I am aware of the sun's warmth on my face and the gratefulness in my heart that on this day I am alive. Looking back one more time at the green stillness rolling over the hill, I exit the cemetery gates more aware of how I want to spend my time on this earth than ever before. Although it would be another year following my visit to Neil's burial site before I would be inspired to write the catchphrase *Drive-Thru, Make It Your Own®,* I can look back on that day and clearly see how the very intent of what it means to drive through life and make it your own experience was born. Unaware at the time, but this marked a tipping point in my life.

*TIPPING POINT*

There will come a moment for all of us where the distance between what we used to do in our youth and what we are able to do right now become insurmountable. This is a tipping point and signals a pivotal moment in time where everything from that point on is as much about reinterpretation as it is acceptance.

For many Baby Boomers there is a never-ending series of tipping points. All sorts of life-altering experiences arrive at our doorstep, symbolizing the end of one stage of our life and the beginning of a new one. Each one feels more important than the last. Choosing which memories to keep and what to let go is a losing battle. The only thing we can do is reinterpret what it means to be youthful in the present moment and accept the obvious passing of time. When we accept our present state of youthful exuberance there is too much fun to worry about what kind of life we used to have.

To look at our present life and know this is as young as we'll ever be grants us the freedom to no longer gauge our joy or sadness based on what has passed us by. Accepting the lessons of our youth is not easy, though. The journey of our life is wrought with emotional experiences that are indescribable. Some are fearful and traumatizing and others are exhilarating and joyous. In our own distinct ways we struggle with tipping points because they represent the death of long-held beliefs. To lay these beliefs to rest is step into the unknown, which is divorcing our past, once and for all.

Letting go of the past is a hard lesson to learn. One way that has worked for me is seeing the immense cost and pain of tinkering with bits and parts of the past believing in the fantasy this will have an effect on the original outcome. This releases me from believing if only I had done something different the result would have been different, and thus my life would have changed. Truly letting go demands that we accept that the whole experience is over. The struggle to pull the past over a gulf into the present cannot be done. There is no present, no ongoing relationship to alter.

After all of the resistance to surrendering the hold that our youthful memories have over us, what else is there to do but accept the gift of youthful exuberance that comes from letting go of thinking our past is better than the present? For right now is the youngest we will ever be. And this is worthy of a celebration!

*OUR LEGACY*

Our lives are not going to get any better unless we learn how to make each moment better than the last. This can happen for all of us when the idea of "We" replaces the loss of "Me", which is seeing our lives reflected in the joy we can give to others. This shift profoundly changed my life and I know it has done the same for millions of others.

We are a generation who has accomplished so much. In our ambitious pursuit to change the world for the better, we lost sight of what really mattered by chasing after acknowledgment and love in all the wrong places. Today, we can look inward and find what we had seemingly lost years ago. Those days of staring at our reflection in the mirror and frowning on what looked back at us are long gone. It's time to extend love to ourselves knowing our Prince Charming is forever smiling at us from within.

> *It's time to extend love to ourselves knowing our Prince Charming is forever smiling at us from within.*

Knowing there is within us a love that transcends all worldly accomplishments is to go beyond the myths of childhood fantasy. The most beautiful form of success we can achieve in the journey of life is to know our genuine purpose, which is to accept our worthiness of being loved and giving love. Despite how we were raised and what society dictates to us, our purpose and worth is not the job or career we have, nor is it even what we do in the later years of our life. Our lives are also not defined by those people we spend our time with. All accomplishments and people will eventually fade away and then what? How will we define ourselves when all we once used as a benchmark for our self-worth is a memory that can barely contain a moments worth of vivid truth?

The legacy we leave for future generations cannot be debilitating myths, such as age being a social disease or there isn't enough happiness to go around. We surely cannot let the world believe romance is long gone after we turn the corner of 55. It is around that corner of age that so many have been taught to dread. It is here, however, where life becomes more beautiful than ever before. This is because we learned the value of slowing down enough to actually breathe in the remarkable experience that our life offers us.

Breaking the myths that framed our youth is the only way to see what we are experiencing now is better than ever. This is not done with malice, resentment or a sense of loss. It is surrendered with the only thing it can be, which is gratitude for what we have been gifted in our lives. How else do we expect to gracefully dance our way through the final years of our life if not on the path that our gratitude for life paved?

The only thing that can derail our journey and tamper with our legacy is to believe in the lies about what we are capable of doing and being. We will not allow anyone to determine what constitutes our youth; define how beautiful we are or how much we deserve to be loved. The myths, ideas and expectations of youth that the Baby Boomer generation helped the media, advertising and entertainment industries shape were merely window dressing to the ultimate beauty and purpose of our time here on this earth. Now, is the time to say goodbye to what no longer serves us and instead, open ourselves up to a way of living youthfully.

Every step, every experience and every breath we've taken in our life has led us here. If we are to honor our youth and everyone we cherish, it is necessary for the life we live right now to be a reflection of our gratitude for the experiences that delivered us here. And with the sun shining on our youthful face, here is pretty good.

333

Made in the USA
Columbia, SC
14 February 2022

56139960R00183